INSIDE OUT

JOHN LORD

Published for John Lord by
Verité CM Limited,
Unit 2, Martlets Way, Goring Business Park,
Goring-by-Sea, West Sussex BN12 4HF
+44 (0) 1903 241975

email: enquiries@veritecm.com
Web: www.veritecm.com

British Library Cataloguing in Publication Data

A catalogue record for this book is available from the British Library

Scripture quotations are taken from the Holy Bible, New International
Version Anglicised. Copyright © 1979, 1984, 2011 by Biblica, formerly
International Bible Society. Used by permission of Hodder & Stoughton

Publishers, an Hachette UK company. All rights reserved.

Design and Typesetting by Verité CM Ltd

Printed in England

DEDICATION

I dedicate this book to my son Jason who always believed in me but never had the opportunity to read the finished article.

Jason Lord

ACKNOWLEDGEMENTS

Without God, this book would never have been possible. I give God all the thanks, all the praise and all the glory for His amazing love and grace that He's shown throughout my life.

I wish to thank the following people for their support in enabling this book to become reality:

Carl & Rachel Portsmouth who are incredibly gifted in their ministry for God and have supported me from the beginning.

John Stewart for the gift and friendship and belief that this book will change people's lives.

Paul & Sian Hobson my Pastors from The Riveria Christian Centre for the continued love and support and belief in the ministry the Lord has called me into.

CONTENTS

PREFACE

In October 1987 I found myself locked into a 6ft by 4ft prison cell in Walton Prison. I was in the punishment block at the time which was freezing cold and stank of urine and human excrement. The lights had been turned out for the night and I was left alone with my thoughts. It was a dark night and I had only the moonlight to bring a little light into that dismal place. I remember that I was looking upwards towards the bars and with my head in my hands I found myself asking the question, 'What is life all about?' and then saying, 'Surely, there must be more to life than this?'

I was twenty-three years of age and was at the start of serving a ten-year prison sentence. My whole life had been a complete farce, and as I started to think about my life I realised that it was in a sorry state of affairs. I thought about where I was and all that had happened since I first walked through those prison gates and I wondered to myself whether I'd ever make it out of prison alive. I thought about my family, and the many people I'd hurt and what I'd put them through. No matter which way I looked at things, I realised that I had failed them miserably and that my life was in a complete mess.

I started contemplating the idea of committing suicide because I couldn't see that my life was going anywhere. I didn't see any reason why I should continue living because I'd hurt countless people over the years I had brought misery and devastation into their lives. I'd robbed and stolen, lied and cheated my way through life, and it didn't matter who I hurt along the way. I finally came to the realisation that I had nothing left worth living for unless something dramatic happened in my life that would change everything. I knew that it was impossible to change myself, but I soon had an experience that was so dynamic that it completely turned my life around and sent me in a different direction.

As you read my story I want to be able to take you on a little journey outside those prison walls that you're in at the moment. Hopefully, when you've finished reading my book, it will bring you into a whole new understanding of what it's really like to be TRULY SET FREE. I've been to prison on several occasions in my life but I didn't take that seriously. Prison was a big joke at first, but I eventually ended up going to a maximum-security jail, which I realised was the end of the line for me. I'd had enough of living life recklessly, and I wanted something different. It was while I was inside prison that I had an amazing encounter with God, and since then my life has never been the same again.

*   *   *   *

PART ONE

1. MY STORY

I was born in Manchester and came from a small estate called Ancoats which is about a mile from the city centre. The environment that I grew up in was well known for its high crime rate, drug abuse and violence. Although Ancoats is a relatively small estate compared to other places like Moss Side and Cheetham Hill, it still holds a record for being one of the most violent areas in Manchester. I made an entrance into this world in the early part of the 1960's at the same time as The Beatles started to become famous and J.F.K was assassinated. It was an era when large families were very popular. I have four sisters and two brothers which, including myself and both my parents, made nine of us in our little family.

I spent the first part of my life living in a three-bedroom council house in Ridgeway Street on the Ancoats estate. I shared a tiny bedroom which most people would call a box-room along with my two brothers James and Karl. It was just big enough to fit in a small wardrobe, one bedside cabinet, and two small bunk beds. James was a year older than me, he was my big brother who had a natural gift for chatting up the girls and making people laugh. He was always the joker at home and would make everybody laugh with some of the stories he came up with, which we called 'add-ons'.

Although he told some amazing stories he hardly told the truth about anything, and that's the reason why he got the name 'Billy Liar' which, funnily enough, was also the name of a TV programme running at that time. The character playing the part in Billy Liar was almost identical to my brother. James was also known as a prolific thief because he would steal almost anything that wasn't nailed down. He gained the reputation of having loose fingers, so he also became known as 'the Thief'.

I had a love-hate relationship with my older brother and had a fearful respect for him but it was the opposite for Karl who was a year younger than me. He was called 'Mouse' because when we were kids we found some white dog mess which we wrapped it up nice and neatly inside a Milky Bar wrapper. (one thing you need to know is that 'Mouse' would always gobble up his food and sweets like a dog eating its last supper). It was hilariously funny to watch him swallow half of the contents before realising what he had eaten. So, from that moment on he used to sniff his food all the time and was pretty quiet around the house. I remember we were always fighting and arguing with each other over everything and anything. It was a pattern of living that followed us right through our younger lives. I was usually quiet at home at the best of times I would try and keep myself out of the limelight. However, whenever I did something wrong I would usually get a beating from my older brother James, it was also the same with Karl who would receive the same treatment.

My four sisters shared a much bigger room at the front of the house and my parents had the largest room at the rear. Tina was my eldest sister, she would keep us all in check while mum and dad weren't around. We used to call her 'Rabbit' because she had buck teeth at the time. It's a name that's stuck with her throughout her life even though she has beautiful teeth now; it's a little private joke which on occasion the family would use. Donna was the second eldest in the family and had a fiery temper. She was quite small for her age and hated being called 'Dwarf' but it's a name that stuck even to this day. Paula, on the other hand, was the complete opposite and although she was quiet in nature she had a mysterious side to her which was quite appealing. Needless to say, she had a family pet name too: 'Sooty' this was mainly because she wasn't that tidy with her personal things around the house.

Last but not least, is my baby sister Joanne who was the youngest in the family. She was a beautiful baby when she was born and we were all very excited to have this new addition to our family. She became less popular though at home when everybody realised that she received most of the attention from mum and dad. The novelty of having a new sister soon wore off and everybody just carried on being a family. I felt sorry for my little sister as she had to grow up very quickly because of this, she always acted a lot older than she was. It was funny because at times she was like a little old woman so we called her 'Granny'.

My dad worked at a chemical factory in Manchester called Clayton Aniline. He worked shifts and was in the same job for over twenty-five years. At the time, it was a well-paid job, but with working with so many different chemicals it had its dangers. Although every precaution was taken to prevent any accidents occurring there was always that danger of a chemical leak or sudden explosion in the factory. It was a dangerous job but dad really enjoyed working there.

Whenever my dad worked the evening shifts he would work long hours into the night and when he finally came home we would hardly see him as during the day he was asleep. Most of our time during the days as spent with mum. Dad, he used to like his drink and would spend lots of time in the pub with his friends whilst he wasn't working. When he first met with mum he was himself in and out of trouble with the police and, on occasion, would spend short spells in prison. When my parents married, my dad stayed out of trouble and started to settle down.

There were times when dad's work took him away from home which meant that we wouldn't see him for several months. It was during this time that mum would struggle to bring up seven kids on her own. She worked hard and held down two part-time jobs as a cleaner along with running a rather hectic home. It wasn't an easy task for her but mum was a real workaholic in those days she always wanted her us kids to look smart and to wear good clothes. I can't remember a time really during those early years when we didn't have what we needed. She kept a good clean home and although at times life seemed to be difficult for us we never seemed to be without.

My mum had her own circle of friends and she would often find herself having a social drink in the local pub. During the school holidays, whole families from the estate would get together in the local pub they would spend most of the day socialising together. While the adults were busy talking and drinking, us kids would normally be playing pool or scrounging money off the drunks to buy sweets and drinks for ourselves. It was a part of everyday life and in a way, we were one big happy family. There would be the usual always arguments and fighting going on in the afternoon when the alcohol started flowing more freely, but most of the time the arguments were amongst family members who were just letting off a bit of steam. In every pub, the landlords were very strict about any fighting in the bars and would soon have things under control if any trouble started.

*   *   *   *

2

GANGS ON THE ESTATE

Manchester was an Aladdin's Cave for thieves and robbers. Its many thousands of factories, shops and warehouses provided many an opportunity for thieves to strike at night or even during the day. There was never a moment when we weren't thinking about burgling somewhere. Whether it was a shop or a factory, it didn't really matter as long as we cleaned the place out of all its contents. We had a constant stream of buyers on the estate who were waiting in the background and were willing to take the goods straight out of our hands at really silly prices. That didn't matter to us because it was quick and easy money to be made and if we were paid in cash we didn't really care.

Life on the Ancoats estate had acquired a reputation for itself over the years. It hadn't always been like that though, because back in the early 60s it was well known for its high success rate in the cotton industry and many canals. It started to lose its veneer back in the late seventies when drugs became more and more available. Although drugs were around at the time, it was only on a small scale in comparison to other parts of the city like the notorious Moss Side and Cheetham Hill areas. Cannabis, acid and speed were quite commonplace. It wasn't until the early eighties that heroin and crack cocaine were introduced onto the estates.

We used to hang around the street corners in gangs and were always getting into trouble with the police, drinking alcohol and smoking cannabis was accepted as part of everyday life. Everybody messed around with drugs in some form or another. Sniffing glue and aerosol cans was another form of entertainment to pass the time of day. We would often get bored with just standing around on the street corners and often we would think of something that was more interesting to do with our time. Some nights we would go looking for trouble and start fights with other gangs on the estate. Somebody always got injured when this happened – if it wasn't a bottle being broken over your head, it could be anything ranging from a knife wound or a metal bar being smashed into your skull. We terrorised the neighbourhood with threats of violence and we would threaten anybody who dared to complain or tried to involve the police. Usually bricks would be flying and crashing through people's windows without warning if they tried to interfere.

Apart from playing football on the local greens and hanging around the street corners you could guarantee that there would always be something happening around the corner. Nearly every day of the week cars were stolen and raced around on the estates. When they weren't being driven around for fun they were being used for other purposes such as ram raids on the local factories or shops. When they had served their purpose, 90 per cent of the time you would find the car burning on some waste ground. The police would hardly ever catch the culprits because they always arrived too late.

On occasion, they might get lucky with a phone call, but it was very rare that they would actually catch anybody committing the offence.

Where I lived, there weren't any facilities to cater for the needs of young people in the community. There were no sports centres around where we lived and even though we went swimming at the local swimming baths, the novelty was short lived because the places were so dilapidated that they were eventually forced to close down because of public safety issues. We used to love swimming in the local canals nearby and would often sit and watch the many barges that would sail past us to unknown destinations. It was great fun until a young lad dived off a large bridge and was impaled on a twelve-foot spike that was sticking out of the water. After that incident, I can't remember ever swimming in the canals again.

The local authorities weren't interested in helping people in the community even though the environment was falling to pieces all around. There were real social issues with regards to crime, alcohol and drugs that weren't being addressed at that time which only made life more unbearable for the people who lived in that area. I remember the council wouldn't acknowledge or accept the seriousness and scale of the drugs problem that was rapidly growing on their own doorstep. Crime, drugs and violence were the only forms of entertainment for young people living on the Ancoats estate and it was on the streets where all this took place.

*   *   *   *

3

IN THE BEGINNING

I started smoking cigarettes when I was around eleven years of age. Both my parents smoked like trains so it wasn't difficult to sneak some 'ciggies' out of their packets without them noticing. At that early age, I could take it or leave it so I didn't take smoking seriously until a couple of years later when I was in my early teens. I had started to dabble with other things like inhaling the gasses from aerosol cans and sniffing glue, which I didn't particularly like doing. There was a lot of peer pressure at the time and, not wanting to feel left out with everyone, we seemed to experiment with most things together.

My first real introduction to drugs was when my friend had tried to commit suicide one day. His girlfriend had finished with him so he drank a full bottle of cider and swallowed a handful of tablets (mainly Valium). I was curious and watched him and waited to see what would happen, but he didn't die. Instead I noticed that he got as high as a kite. I recall finding that funny and so I decided to join him in his suicide pact by swallowing a load of my mum's sleeping tablets that I'd found in the cupboard at home. I swallowed the tablets and washed them down with half a bottle of cider. After that I can't remember much about that night, other than we were both stoned out of our heads and lived to tell the tale.

It became a ritual between us and I know it sounds crazy, but at least once a week we would get as many tablets as we could find and, with a bottle of cider or spirits, we would find somewhere private where we could get off our heads.

*   *   *   *

4

BONFIRE NIGHT

November 5th, Bonfire Night, was always a great time for us as kids. We would start collecting wood for the bonfire weeks in advance so that we would have the biggest bonfire around. The local council tried to ban Bonfire Night from happening because wherever there was an empty property there were always gangs of youths around who would strip it bare like locusts. Whole kitchens, including the wooden floors, were completely ransacked and destroyed within a matter of minutes. New or used doors were ripped off their hinges, and anything that was made of wood was also torn apart and hauled off to the nearest bonfire.

There was a time when we were searching for wood one day in the back yards of people's homes when we came across a coffin-like box which was just lying around, leaning against a brick wall. There were no occupants of the property at the time so we knew that the house was empty. It wasn't long before we lobbed the box over the wall and were parading it through the streets. We pretended it was a real funeral procession and the neighbours came out of their homes to see what was happening. Some people just stared in disbelief at the spectacle while others would shout something and cheer us on. It must have looked a funny sight to say the least but we weren't too bothered as we were having a whale of a time.

When we finally arrived at the bonfire site, I remember sitting down on some old settees that we'd collected and we were smoking cannabis and drinking beer. Somebody volunteered to lie down in the coffin as a joke pretending to be dead, which seemed really funny at the time. He lay down and folded his arms like Count Dracula and, without giving him to chance to escape, we closed the coffin lid and nailed it shut. After a few minutes inside he started frantically banging on the wood hollering to be let out, but we were enjoying ourselves too much and soon forgot that he was inside. We turned the music up louder and started partying.

It wasn't until about half an hour later that we decided to have an early Bonfire Night. So, with the music blaring, into the night sky, and the cannabis and drink flowing freely, an old petrol can was left lying about. Somebody started throwing petrol onto the wood and even dousing the coffin with splashes of petrol. In the process a match was struck and the bonfire was started to burn along nicely. The fire quickly turned to blaze when unwittingly someone picked up a piece of burning wood he threw it in the direction of the coffin which was like lighting a candle. Within seconds it was burning brightly into the night sky.

Fortunately, someone had heard the screaming coming from the burning box. It was starting to look more like a charred mess of black charcoal. We managed to drag the coffin away from the main bonfire and soon put the fire out enough to flip the lid open and rescue our friend inside. It was sheer luck for him that the box hadn't burnt right through. But enough of the flames and smoke had penetrated the holes that were appearing through the wood to start singeing and burning most of his clothes.

Nobody knew what to expect when we prised open the coffin lid as the poor lad had nearly been cremated on the spot. It was like watching a scene from '*The Rocky Horror Show* 'when he leapt out like a little jack-in-the-box. Needless to say, he was hysterical, shouting and swearing at everybody until he realised that he wasn't badly hurt after all. By this time everybody was laughing and cheering spontaneously at the whole spectacle and. after a little while longer, he managed to calm down and soon started to join in with the joke and see the funny side of things.

*   *   *   *

5

THE AEROPLANE

W̶e stole an aeroplane from an old scrap yard near the city centre. There was a gang of us scrummaging around in the old knacker's yard. We were having a great time smashing up the old cars which were piled on top of each other. It was a scrap dealer's nightmare because there was several thousand pounds' worth of damage caused on the property. The carnage continued throughout the day and it was by chance that we came across a private jet hidden in the warehouse next door. Whether it was there to be used for scrap or repair I couldn't say, but it didn't take us long to decide what to do. After securing the wings and the front end of the plane with rope and chains we pulled the jet out into an open space where we could inspect it more thoroughly.

It appeared to be in a good condition, we had great fun for most of the day pretending to be the pilots of an aircraft who were out on a special mission. It became more realistic when somebody suggested that we snap the lock on the main gates and fly the plane out in the open road. It didn't take long for twenty of us to pull the light aircraft onto the main road in the city centre. People were watching with amused looks, but weren't sure of our intentions until we positioned the plane at the top of a very steep hill. We had all jumped on board and the plane started to roll down the hill, slowly at first, but then it gradually started to pick up speed as we descended the hill. It was a nightmare scenario that was becoming a reality especially for the oncoming traffic.

The main road was at least forty-feet wide and held two lanes on either side. Although the body of the private aircraft was quite small it still had a huge wing span which meant that when the plane was positioned on the main road it looked a lot bigger than we'd originally thought. Once we started to pick up speed we realised that we had no real control over the steering of the plane from the cockpit. It was accelerating at a fast pace and to the onlooker it must have looked quite a bizarre scene because we were hanging onto the wings; as we were moving towards the traffic we were shouting abuse and making rude gestures to the passers-by.

We were all piled high into the cockpit and we watched with amusement the oncoming traffic as it was skidding across the road in all directions to avoid a collision. A double-decker bus was driving towards us and I can remember the horror on the passengers' faces as we headed straight towards them. It was hilarious to us, but for the traffic that was coming and going in different directions, they didn't see the funny side.

The fun finally came to an end when, at a considerable speed, the aeroplane smashed into the traffic lights at the bottom of the road. Everybody was still intact and, apart from a few cuts and bruises, we'd had a brilliant time. We eventually bailed out and ran off laughing into the nearby estate to escape the police who were fast approaching.

*   *   *   *

6

MUM EXPLOSION

One Sunday afternoon mum was busy preparing the potatoes and vegetables for the Sunday roast. It was a lovely day and while she was organising the rest of the food, a couple of my mates called around with some weed to smoke. We sat around the house watching TV while mum was rushing about the kitchen trying to get everything sorted out for the family dinner.

When she had, everything prepared she said that she was just popping out to visit a friend. Before she left the house, she reminded me not to forget to turn the cooker on at 2.00pm. I said that I wouldn't forget, but when she left I continued smoking and talking with my mates and I soon forgot all about it. The phone rang, it was my mum telling me she was on her way home.

I was feeling a little stoned at the time, so when I went into the kitchen I couldn't remember why I was there. When it finally came to me, I remember I turned the gas on but I forgot to light it. It was around fifteen minutes later when mum came home and straight away she started complaining that she could smell gas coming from the kitchen. I didn't notice it at the time but she had a lit cigarette hanging from her mouth when she walked into the kitchen. I could hear that she was muttering something under her breath and the next thing I can remember was a sudden flash, followed by a large explosion. Everybody looked in the direction of the kitchen and the next thing we saw was my mum flying across the room and being lifted around four feet in the air.

I don't know whether it was through shock or the effects of the cannabis, but I'd never seen anything like it. All I can remember is that I was laughing like an idiot when she came staggering into the room with hardly any hair at the front of her head. I laughed even more when I realised that she had no eyebrows left and was stood motionless in the doorway with the cigarette still hanging in her mouth. It seemed so surreal and I know that I should have reacted differently but I wasn't in the right frame of mind at the time.

Obviously, it was the affects from the cannabis, but as serious as the situation was at the time I just couldn't take it seriously enough. Dad had been working nights and was upstairs in bed, as soon as he heard the explosion he jumped up and ran downstairs. When he realised what had happened he launched himself across the room and he gave me a real leathering (which I thoroughly deserved by the way). Poor mum was shaking for weeks afterwards.

*   *   *   *

PART TWO

7. THE CLAYTON WARS

As far as I can remember, at least once a year the local street gangs would join from different estates and would battle it out in the open fields. It became known as the Clayton Wars where blood and guts were spilled out onto the fields. It was violence at its worst. Guns, axes, knives and machetes were the usual weapons used. We also often used crossbows, bottles, bricks and petrol bombs. The battle usually took place in a small valley in Clayton which was difficult for the police to reach by road. It was total chaos and there were never really any winners from either side. I guess it was just another way of venting our frustrations through boredom.

The gangs from Newton Heath, Miles Platting and Ancoats would join together at the abattoir which was behind the Philips Park Cemetery off Briscoe Lane. It was like being at a football match but the difference was that we weren't there to watch football; we were there with the sole purpose of fighting. When everybody had arrived up at the meeting place we would then make our way towards the valley where there were gangs of youths from Clayton and Openshaw already waiting for us to arrive. There was a small bridge which separated the two sides from meeting together. Whenever the fighting had started nobody could cross this line because it was usually blocked and barricaded with burnt cars from both sides.

The fighting would usually start in the morning and would continue for several hours. Gangs from both sides would shout abuse at each other. On occasion, there would be youths who would race down into the valley on motor bikes as though it was a jousting competition. Somebody always got injured; there were heavy casualties from both sides. It definitely wasn't for the faint hearted, especially one day in particular when one of the gang members from Newton Heath was caught and dragged across the field. The young lad was captured around midday by some youths and was beaten up quite severely. He was dragged across the field and finally nailed to the bridge.

The police were watching all this take place from a distance. They tried to intervene at the time, but they were continually being held back by youths who were retaliating by throwing bricks, bottles and other dangerous missiles in their direction which prevented them from reaching the youth straight away. The police finally broke through all the carnage and rescued a young boy who was rushed to the nearest hospital. We heard later in the day that he was going to be alright and would make a good recovery. After this incident, I, don't believe there was ever any more fighting in the valley and that was the last that I heard of the Clayton Wars.

*   *   *   *

8

THE JELLY BABY GANG

One night we stole a car from the outskirts of Manchester and drove around on the Ancoats estate where we would show off to the girls who used to hang around the street corners. That night I remember it was some of the worst weather that I'd seen for a long time. It was throwing it down with rain and gusts of winds over 60 mph. The weather was so bad that slates were being blown off the roofs of houses and many gates and garden fences were uprooted and tossed around as though they were in the middle of a mini tornado.

Debris was flying everywhere; however, that didn't stop us from driving around as though we were in a demolition derby. There was a briefcase on the passenger seat of the car which created quite a bit of interest until we realised that there was no money inside. Without a second thought it was thrown out of the car window and disappeared into the night along with all its contents which were blown all over the street. We finally ran out of petrol and dumped the car in a dark alley alongside a pub thinking that nobody would find it until the next day.

We all decided to go back to my friend's house. We all sat around smoking cannabis and having a laugh when suddenly, the front door of the house literally came off its hinges and in walked three burly men who we'd

31

never seen before. Everybody was in total shock and nobody moved for a while. But then my mate leapt to his feet and confronted the intruders, shouting, 'Who do you think you are?' One of the men asked quite calmly, 'Have you ever heard of the Quality Street Gang?' And, without any hesitation my mate replied, 'No, have you ever heard of the 'Jelly Baby Gang?' He was about to jump into a fight when quite matter-of-factly a sawn-off shotgun appeared out of nowhere and was pointed directly into his face.

This changed things considerably and everybody from that moment on gave their undivided attention to the men stood in the room. We hadn't heard of the Quality Street Gang but we later discovered that these men were part of the gang that was known as the 'real' gangsters in Manchester. They ran the city. We were told that the car had been found, but that this was of no real concern to them. However, it was the briefcase that was inside which was of great importance to them. In no uncertain terms, they threatened that if the briefcase with all its contents wasn't returned within the hour the consequences for all of us would be unimaginably painful.

How they found out where we were and who rumbled us about the car wasn't in question. We found the briefcase straight away, but its contents were spread all over the estate. After several hours of searching and chasing through the rain and wind swept streets we collected most of what was inside the briefcase. Soaked to the skin we went back to the house and from then on, as punishment we had to work alongside these men to make up for stepping onto their territory. Every decent car we stole had to be parked outside the car lot in Ancoats Lane where they would be reconditioned and sold to prospective buyers as a legitimate sale.

*   *   *   *

9

THE ACCIDENT

I had a serious accident at the age of fourteen which put me out of school for over a year. Looking back, I'd say that it played a deciding factor in the direction to which way my life would take from there.

I was committing a burglary at a warehouse with a gang of youth. While I was passing boxes of stolen goods down the ladder a security guard appeared and flashed his light before the window. I shouted to my friends that we'd been sussed out and before you could say 'Black Mariah' everybody had scampered off the rooftop in different directions.

I was the last man standing and was starting to panic because I was still at the top of a very tall ladder. The security guard had raised the alarm on his radio and I knew it would only be a matter of time before the police arrived. So, in my haste to get away I practically slid down the ladder like a fireman in a burning building. I tried to make my escape across the rooftop as fast as my legs would carry me, but it was starting to get dark and the visibility was quite bad. I continued to run in the direction of where my friends had scarpered and kept on tripping and falling along the broken glass which was strewn across the rooftop.

While I was looking for a way of escape I noticed that there was a small wall ahead and, without looking or thinking what was on the other side, I vaulted over it. I caught my foot on a piece of barbed wire which was protruding from the edge. It all happened so quickly, the last thing I can remember I was falling from a height of around forty-five feet and found myself crashing head first through a sky-light window in the adjacent building. I smashed through the lighting and beams and I eventually landed head first on a concrete floor.

Although my friends had already made their escape, they were still standing at a distance on the canal edge and were laughing and throwing bricks at the security guard. It was sheer luck that one of my friends had witnessed my crashing through the roof and while he was stood around waiting for me to appear through the dust and debris, he didn't realise that I was seriously injured. Others had started to hang around but when they heard the sound of the police sirens drawing closer they decided to make their getaway and ran off into the nearest estate. When my mate realised that I wasn't coming out he knew that something was wrong and he ran across the estate to my parents' house to break the news.

Both my parents were at home at the time and when they heard somebody shouting and banging at the front door they immediately knew that there had been an accident. My mum finally opened the door and with all the noise and shouting she nearly collapsed when she heard somebody shout, 'Hurry, Mrs Lord, your son is dead, he's been killed in the Old Mill factory.'

Dad tried to calm everybody down and attempted to make sense of what had happened. Through all the commotion he started to piece together what had taken place and ran through the front door. Mum was in terrible shock and was running through the streets screaming hysterically thinking that her son was dead. It wasn't long before they arrived at the Old Mill where there were police cars surrounding the building, an ambulance which was already in attendance and even a fire engine that was called to the scene.

While the police were looking for an opening in the derelict building my dad ran alongside and explained to them about the accident and pointed out the spot where they were told I'd fallen through the roof. The Old Mill had been closed for several years and although it was fenced off from the public and the windows were boarded up, it didn't stop the gangs of youths from breaking into the place and wreaking havoc inside. On several occasions parts of the building had been set on fire and everything inside was smashed to smithereens. It was a dangerous place for anybody to venture into and there had been many incidents in the past where young people were injured. (The local authorities had eventually intervened and decided to condemn the building to be demolished.)

The police finally located where I was and it was there that they saw my lifeless body. I was lying in a crumpled heap with blood pouring from my nose, mouth and ears. I was quite motionless and as I lay there my eyes were wide open. It appeared to everybody that I was definitely dead, but it was soon realised on closer inspection that I was still breathing. I was rushed to the nearest hospital and was placed on a life support machine where, for over two weeks, I was left in a coma. The doctors at the hospital weren't sure if I'd pull through from the accident. Mum and dad were totally distraught with what had happened and didn't really know what to do apart from pray and hope for a miracle.

The serious injuries were around my head where there were a number of fractures so severe that it was almost impossible and far too dangerous for the surgeons to operate. I was like Humpty Dumpty: a broken egg and nobody could put me back together again. The doctors couldn't do anything else but wait and see what would happen. It was a matter of life and death, and in their opinion they held out little hope for a full recovery. I seemed to lapse further and further into the coma. There were no improvements in my condition and, as my situation became more desperate, my parents finally had to come to terms with the reality of what they were faced with. There was a strong possibility that I was going to die and they had to make a decision. So, reluctantly, they decided to contact the local priest and asked him to perform the last rites over me.

It was against all the odds that I woke up one day, even though I didn't know it at the time, I now realise that God had definitely put His hand of protection over my life. When I woke up from the coma my mind was in total disarray and I couldn't remember anything about what had happened. The doctors had told my parents that I'd suffered serious head injuries through the accident and that the possibility of a full recovery was unlikely.

My parents were advised by the doctors that there would be many difficult times ahead and that any improvement in my condition would be nothing short of a miracle. My journey to recovery started and during my convalescence I suffered constantly with severe headaches and blackouts. I was told that this was a normal reaction and that in due course those things would improve.

I spent three months in the hospital trying to recuperate after the accident. I was like a little child in my mind and had to learn how to walk and talk again. My whole world had fallen apart in that one moment when I fell through the roof of the building. I was constantly frustrated with my inability to do even the most basic things in life but I was determined not to allow myself to be beaten by it. While I was still at the hospital I had regular physiotherapy sessions, visits by numerous doctors, neurologists and surgeons who were all involved with my rehabilitation.

It was at times like this that I appreciated having such a large family and so many good friends. There was never a dull moment with my brothers and sisters visiting the hospital almost every day. My whole family were like vigilantes by my side, urging me to get better. It made me feel like royalty being given so much attention. The feeling was short lived as the doctors called my parents one day and told them that there was nothing more they could do and that I was soon to be sent home from the hospital.

The next few months in my life were a real nightmare. I was struggling with bouts of depression, banging headaches and a lack of memory. I'd never suffered from depression in my life before, I was always a happy-go-lucky type of person but when the depression started, it hit me like a ton of bricks. Sometimes I felt desperately low in my spirits and on occasion I would feel like giving up on life completely. I couldn't seem to fit back into normal life anymore and I started to lose interest in what was going on around me. It was during that time of depression that I would often sink into a world of my own. I would sit around the house and while all the usual noises of everyday life were going on around me I found that I was living in a completely different world.

I tried to study at home to keep up with my school work but I couldn't really concentrate on anything for too long. Instead, I would walk around the streets hanging out with my mates who played truant from school quite a lot. We would often get into trouble and frequently visited the city centre where we would steal almost anything that would provide us with some money. On occasion, we would get caught, we were either thrown out of the stores or the police were called and we would be taken home to face our parents. I was more afraid of facing my dad than the police and would always try to lie my way out of things. Sometimes the police would call my dad at work so that he had to come to the police station to pick me up. I'd be terrified of going home because I knew that I was going to get the belt. My father was very strict and a no-nonsense type of man. He worked hard to support his family and here I was, being totally selfish in just throwing it all back in his face.

Sometimes I would be sitting at home and my mind would go completely blank. It was happening on a regular basis and I started to get really depressed. I didn't talk to anybody about the way I was feeling which made things even worse because I had a real tendency to bottle things up inside of me for long periods of time. I was like a box of Rice Krispies: snap, crackle and pop. I'd fly off the handle at every opportunity that I could and I didn't care who I hurt along the way. It was the same at home with my brothers and sisters; I was constantly fighting and arguing with them too.

I realise now that there was as a real battle taking place inside of me. I know that my violent behaviour and mood swings had a lot to do with the accident and, looking back at it now, I realise that I needed therapy and counselling. But none of those options were available to me at the time so I was left to deal with things in my own way. Although I'd been sent home from the hospital it was another nine months before I went back to school. I'd literally missed out on a full year's education. When I finally did return, it seemed so strange and I felt completely out of place. Too much time had elapsed and I just couldn't be bothered trying to catch up with my schoolwork. Instead, I found myself making up excuses to my teachers and even lied to my parents about how I felt. I even used my accident as an excuse about how I was feeling and would eventually play truant whenever I could.

I would often cause fights with other pupils at school and would look for every opportunity to get myself expelled. I remember whacking my best mate unconscious one day without feeling any remorse. Although I knew that it was totally out of character for me to do something like that, I started to enjoy seeing other people being hurt. I was expelled from school for two weeks for that episode but that was fine by me because that's just exactly what I wanted. I was angry, frustrated and seemed to lash out at every opportunity. In my anger, I started to turn against the very people that loved me. I was beginning to resent my parents for trying to keep me in school and for not understanding what I was going through. I even tried to blame them for anything that wasn't going right in my life. My poor parents were getting the brunt of my frustrations and it wasn't even their fault.

During my last twelve months at school I was expelled more times than I can remember. My parents kept on pleading with the headmaster to give me another chance. With a little more persuasion, the school agreed to let me stay, but nothing had changed from my perspective. In my mind, I was gradually getting worse and continued with my outbursts of violence. It was with some reluctance and relief also from the school board that I was eventually expelled permanently from the school. It didn't matter to me whether I went to school or not but my parents were so disappointed and upset by this. I concluded in my mind that the education system could no longer do anything for me. So, without taking any final exams and receiving no qualifications whatsoever, I finally left school at the age of fifteen.

*　　*　　*　　*

10

STARTING WORK

I started to look for work and soon found a job assembling prams at a local factory near the city centre. It was a well-paid job but I found it was quite tedious work and soon became bored. I wasn't satisfied with being cooped up in a factory like a chicken all day long. So, after working at the factory for just eight weeks, I finally decided to try something else and handed in my notice. Wherever I worked, and whoever my employers were, I wouldn't stay for too long in any job because as soon as I had worked out the easiest way of sneaking past the security, I would quit my job and would usually break into the place that same day.

I found that it was a quick way of making money and I soon realised that I could earn more money in an hour stealing than I would by working a full forty hours a week. I would often dream of making large amounts of money and driving around the estate in nice fancy cars. I knew that this wasn't going to happen while I was working a 9-to-5 job. It was around about this time that I decided which was a whole lot easier and more profitable all round if I lived a life of crime.

I was making good money now, I enjoyed the attention and the respect that I was getting from my friends. It felt good, not taking orders from people and not being accountable to anybody else. It was like being your own boss, and having nobody to answer to suited me just fine. I felt as though I was in control of my own destiny and I wasn't going to allow anybody to get in my way. Over the years, I had developed a stinking attitude towards anyone in a position of authority. I didn't understand politics, but I did have my own views on life as far as I was concerned everybody was corrupt in some form or other.

*   *   *   *

11

BILLY THE KID

Not long after I left school I bought a hand gun from a friend and I was keen to try it out. It was a semi-automatic that I paid around £50 for. I thought that I'd go and find some place quiet where I could practice with the gun without being disturbed. There was an old site nearby where there were some derelict buildings. I decided that I'd go there for some target practice. I walked out of my parents' home early in the morning feeling as though I was walking on air. I had the gun tucked away inside of my jacket and I could feel the cold metal pressing against my body. I was feeling a little nervous but that soon passed as I noticed my friend Sam hanging around innocently on the street corner. I called his name and when he recognised me he gave a short wave and started to walk in my direction. I thought that I'd show off my new gun and when he was about thirty yards away I automatically raised my arm and pointed the gun in his direction and fired a shot.

Wow, cool, I thought to myself, it works. But then panic started to kick in because, before I realised what was happening, my mate was on the floor with blood oozing from the side of his head. While all this was going on my dad had heard the screaming from inside the house and ran out into the street. I remember I being dragged into the house and given a good beating.

Fortunately for me, and even more fortunately for my friend, the bullet had whizzed past the side of his head and had just caught the bottom half of his left ear lobe. It wasn't as serious as I thought and it was soon sorted out at the hospital with a few stitches. My dad took the gun away from me that day and disposed of it quickly. Although I felt gutted about this I also felt a little relieved at the same time.

*   *   *   *

12

DRUGS GALORE

I was always curious about my brother James who would disappear most evenings through the bedroom window when everybody was asleep in bed. So, one night, I deliberately stayed awake, fully dressed under the blankets, waiting for him to disappear into the night. I heard him going out of the window and like a cat on a hot tin roof I was soon following close behind. He met up with a friend of his and they started to walk away quickly, they were laughing and joking along the way. I managed to keep him in my sights until he came to a block of maisonettes which was around the corner. I watched as he rang the doorbell and when the door was finally opened they went inside and I was left outside wandering what to do next.

I didn't know the person who lived there and was debating whether I should return home. But curiosity certainly had hold of me this time and I thought what the heck, I'll just give it a try. I built up my courage to knock on the door and when it was finally opened I just stood there and didn't know what to say at first. Then I asked for my brother. When he came to the door he threatened to beat me up if I didn't leave. I was determined to find out what all the excitement was about so with a little pleading and a hint of blackmail I managed to persuade my bro to let me stay. You've heard the saying 'curiosity killed the cat but satisfaction brought him back'. I had my first line of speed that night and not even a locomotive train could have moved me away from there.

It soon became my second home. Almost every night over the next two years I called around Steve's house. I soon found out that it was one of the biggest drugs dens in Miles Platting. Drug dealers would travel from all over the country to buy and sell drugs in the kilos. Whether it was amphetamines, cocaine, or even heroin, it was guaranteed that it would always arrive in large quantities. It was an introduction to life in the fast lane and I loved the excitement of living this double life. At night, I would sneak through the bedroom window and live the life of Riley, but I would return home in the early hours before anybody noticed that I was missing.

There were always parties going on with plenty of drugs, booze and women available. I remember the fights that used to take place there which were a real buzz to watch – although it was very frightening to be around. There was always somebody who thought that they were bigger than everybody else – hence the reason why lots of people carried guns around for their own protection. Sometimes it seemed like you were actually taking part in a western movie except it was for real. It was a different world altogether and I just happened to be smack bang in the middle of it all.

It wasn't long before my little addiction to speed started to grow bigger. Every drug that was on the market came through that house. All the main drug dealers in Manchester would meet together to buy and sell whatever drugs that were available. I became the sky pilot who tested everything that was on offer (free, of course) which was usually cannabis, amphetamines, heroin or cocaine. I was like a human fertiliser and I couldn't get enough. I wasn't too keen on heroin and kept away from it for a number of years. However, that too eventually caught up with me, and was one of the main reasons why I lost the plot and ended up going to prison later in life.

Although I'd committed hundreds of burglaries on factories, shops and offices with my friends, I preferred to work on my own. This way I didn't have to worry about what anybody would say if they were arrested. It was very rare that I'd be caught doing anything while I worked on my own, whether it was in the evening or even during the day. I started breaking into safes and on many occasions, would come away with considerable amounts of money which helped maintain not only my addiction to drugs but also my lifestyle pertaining to the drugs scene.

*   *   *   *

PART THREE

13. NEWHALL DETENTION CENTRE

I was eighteen when I was arrested for a burglary and given a three-month custodial sentence at Newhall Detention Centre in Leeds. It was an old army base which was run by ex-army officers. In the early eighties, there was a general outcry by the public for the government to tackle the increase in crime around the country. It had put the government under constant pressure to do something about it and, as part of their promise, they introduced a new system of how to deal with this problem. Newhall was just one of many such establishments that were set up throughout England. When it was introduced it was supposed to be a short, sharp, shock to the offender and was generated to prevent young offenders from re-offending.

It was certainly a shock to the system for most of the young offenders who were being sent there by the magistrates' courts but it didn't work. There were hundreds of inmates who had been through this procedure more than twice and still hadn't learnt their lesson. It was just like water flowing off a duck's back to them and it went without saying that they were the type who would inevitably end up inside prison for most of their adult lives. In my case, it just re-enforced my resolve to get back at the authorities. I started to resent authority more than ever and wanted to get back at them for taking away my freedom.

When I arrived at the detention centre I hated every minute of it and I couldn't wait to get released and be back outside where all the action was. I was already street wise and could handle myself when it came to fighting, so that wasn't a problem, but while I was inside I witnessed lots of fighting and bullying taking place nearly every day.

I managed to keep my head down and get through the sentence without any real problems. I tried to avoid the fighting mainly because I wanted to get out as soon as possible, but a couple of times I ended up getting myself involved in a bit of a scramble to establish myself and warn other inmates to keep their distance. It was a constant drag living with all the strict rules and regulations at Newhall. Every day was basically the same routine and with the same boring military-style drills. Some of the screws weren't too bad, but then there were the authoritarian types who acted like little Hitlers constantly trying to run the inmates into the ground with their petty orders and strict rules.

It was just like being in the army, I supposed, and I was glad that it was only for a short time. I received letters and visits from my family, and would also receive all the news and gossip from my friends. I looked forward to my letters because it kept me in touch with what was happening in the outside world. I promised my parents that it would never happen again and that I would make every effort to go on the straight and narrow when I got released. At the time, I meant it to a certain degree, but I knew in my heart that I couldn't keep that promise.

I was finally released after serving three months inside and I ended up living at my parents' home on Ridgeway Street in Ancoats. It seemed strange living with my parents again because so much had happened in my life since I left. I was feeling quite restless and, within three weeks of my hitting the streets, I found myself slipping back into my old ways. I started hanging around with my old friends who were still up to their usual old tricks like smoking pot, snorting speed, and popping acid tabs like there was no tomorrow. I enjoyed the excitement of living recklessly and it wasn't too long before I joined in with the crowd again. Soon I was blending back into my old way of life.

*   *   *   *

14

SELLING DRUGS

I was living with my girlfriend who became pregnant with my son Jason. We had started selling drugs from my flat on the Ancoats estate which was right next door to a police station; it was literally 200 yards away from my front door. At the time, I was anti heroin and wouldn't entertain the thought of selling the stuff to anybody. My addiction to speed and cocaine was growing by the day and instead of saving money from the proceeds of selling drugs, we were injecting all the profits into our arms. I was still stealing and robbing during the day but the money that I earned doing that only paid for more and more drugs.

In July 1985, my girlfriend was rushed into hospital with a suspected drugs overdose. We had been injecting amphetamines for several days non-stop, day and night, when suddenly, she complained about not feeling too good. I remember her even cracking a joke about the baby being due on that day, I didn't take her seriously because we both knew that she was only seven months into the pregnancy. When we arrived at the hospital, instead of going into the accident and emergency ward she was rushed straight into a delivery room on the labour ward.

At the hospital, the doctors and nurses were rushing around while I stood there wondering what on earth was happening. We were both stoned out of our heads on drugs. While I was waiting in the reception room at the hospital I felt as though I was going to collapse with exhaustion. I was both physically and mentally drained through constant drug abuse over the years. It was a rare moment for me, but I started to think about my life and the direction to which it was going. I was tired of taking drugs and I wondered to myself whether it would be possible to ever break free from a life of addiction.

I started to think about the times when I'd been rushed into hospital myself and had had near death experiences through drugs overdoses, or from any of the many serious car crashes that I'd had in the past. My mind was racing around while I was trying to make sense of everything, I couldn't think straight anymore because of the drugs. I stopped trying to figure out things and started to focus on what was going on at the hospital. It seemed like I was waiting for ages and nobody was telling me what was happening and I started to get impatient with the doctors and nurses. I felt really stressed out by this time and I just wanted to leave, but I knew that I had to stay.

My mind started to wander off again into a different world and I knew that I desperately needed to rest, but I couldn't. I decided to hang around for a while longer but then I started to hallucinate in the hospital and all hell broke loose. There appeared to be demons popping up from out of nowhere and gremlin-like things were running around trying to frighten the life out of me. I realised that I was having a bad trip from the drugs so I rushed into the hospital toilets and had another fix.

A short time later, when I came out of the toilets, the doctor came into the waiting room and said that I was the father of a baby boy.

My girlfriend had a caesarean birth within an hour of being admitted to the hospital. The baby was immediately put into an incubator where he would spend the next two months being weaned off the drugs. Jason was born into this world a drug addict. When I went into the delivery room and saw my girlfriend lying in the hospital bed, it didn't seem as though she'd just given birth to a baby. She said that she needed a fix and I pulled the syringe out of my jacket pocket and gave her an injection. When I finished, I looked towards the new-born baby and thought to myself, 'What on earth have we done?'

The baby wasn't fully developed and I noticed that he had hair like fur all over his little body. It didn't look natural and the fact that I was hallucinating at the time didn't help matters much. I decided that I wanted to go home and thirty minutes later I was sitting in the flat injecting myself with more drugs. I didn't remember anything else because I had totally collapsed on the floor and passed out. I didn't wake up again for two whole days. The next few weeks were a total blur but I can remember going into the hospital and seeing my girlfriend with my son. I was caught up in the world of drug addiction which was impossible to break free from. I felt that I couldn't cope with being a father at that early age and would often find myself returning to the flat feeling rather depressed at the whole situation.

*   *   *   *

15

HMP STRANGEWAYS

My girlfriend was finally allowed home from the hospital and we just continued with our lives as usual. We were still selling drugs from the flat but it wasn't paying for our ever-growing drug addictions. I was drinking heavily and, on top of that, I was injecting at least £300 worth of drugs into my body per day. My partner wasn't that far behind me with her habit that was growing at a faster pace than mine. I felt that I had no choice but to go out and start stealing again. The money that I was earning wasn't enough to cater for our lifestyle. It only lasted for a while and I would be back out looking for more cash. I was taking lots of risks and I knew that sooner or later I would be caught, but I didn't really care because I was so addicted to the drugs. One day I got lucky and hit on a nice little earner. For a while things seemed to be working out financially when suddenly, the flat was raided by the police and I was arrested for an attempted burglary and stealing property from cars in the city centre.

I was brought before the magistrates' courts in Manchester after spending a night in the cells at the Grey Mare Lane police station. This was something which happened on a regular basis so the surroundings were all too familiar when I was escorted into the courtroom by two burly police officers. When the short proceedings commenced, it wasn't long before the court's prosecutor was reading off the most recent charges and was demanding that the local magistrates remanded me in custody without bail. They agreed with the prosecution's argument that the streets would be a lot safer without the likes of me and, because of my track record, the magistrates didn't hesitate in sending me to the infamous Strangeways Prison where I was to be remanded in custody whilst awaiting trial.

After the courts, had finished I was taken down into the cell area was then handcuffed and them shoved into a prison van along with twelve other prisoners. It was only a short journey from the magistrates' courts to the prison. As we were moving along through the busy traffic I was looking out of the small window thinking to myself, 'It's going to be a while before I see the outside world again.' When the prison van finally arrived at Strangeways I was put on the remand wing with the rest of the remand prisoners. It was my first time inside an adult prison and I was not sure what to expect.

Remand prisoners who were awaiting trial and were not yet convicted of any offence had a lot more privileges than those who had been convicted and were serving out their sentences. You could have regular visits every day, even food and tobacco could be brought in along with clothes and other little necessities. I had the occasional visits from my family and friends who kept me up to date with what was going on in the outside world. Although I was on remand life inside the prison seemed pretty much mundane. There was no real structure to the way the prison was being run other than it being a holding centre for those who were awaiting trial.

I heard from my solicitors that they had applied for Judge in Chambers (which was a special court hearing) and because the offences that I'd been charged with were relatively petty there was a strong possibility that I could be released early whilst pending trial. The prospect of being set free made life that much more bearable so I just knuckled down and took things one day at a time.

I was sharing a cell with a Geordie lad who was around about my age at the time which eased things up a little. We seemed to get on all right but I couldn't understand a word that he was saying half of the time because of his accent. He had regular visits and on occasions would have drugs brought in on the visit, along with lots of munchies to eat along the way. We would spend most evenings smoking cannabis in the cell and getting stoned out of our faces.

I'd been cooped up in a stinking cell for the best part of three months and there was still no sign of a court date for my trial (or bail through the Judge in Chambers). It usually took around twelve months for the prosecution to prepare its case along with the gathering of evidence and witness statements. There was such a large contingency of inmates on remand and awaiting trial that the legal profession at times seemed to operate at a snail's pace.

I received a letter one day from my partner which was a 'Dear John' letter. When somebody receives a Dear John letter it's usually a letter from a girlfriend who's simply had enough and wants to end the relationship. Everything had been going well between us up until then, or at least that's what I thought. So, when I received the letter I just wasn't prepared for this and it came as a real shock when she mentioned that she had wanted to end the relationship. We'd been going out with each other for twelve months and I thought the world of her. I just couldn't believe that she was deserting me when I needed her the most.

I read the letter and my head was spinning around inside. I became very angry and within a few minutes I started to smash the cell to pieces, barricading myself inside the cell and I wedged the two beds together against the door. I continued to smash the contents of the cell to smithereens; within minutes I was stood on a chair with one end of a torn bed sheet around my neck and the other end strung around the bars on the window. While all this commotion was going on there was a lot of movement going on outside the cell door. The alarm had been raised and the screws were locking everybody up in their cells whilst they dealt with the situation.

There were several prison officers on the landing outside the cell who were attempting to break through the barricaded door. I could hear somebody shouting through the judas hole (which is a small circular hole in the metal door that allows the screws to look through to make sure you're still there). A prison officer was trying to talk me down but I was determined not to listen and continued to shout abuse and threaten to kill myself. It was seriously starting to get out of control and I could hear the doors were being prised open with jackhammers. Little by little the cell door was being opened like a giant tin opener and I knew it was just a matter of time before they forced entry and would be crawling all over the place.

In a moment of complete madness, I kicked the chair away from underneath my feet and the last thing that I can remember was the doors breaking open and some shouting from the prison officers. Suddenly everything went completely white and I felt at total peace with myself. I can't remember much more about that incident except that when I next opened my eyes I found I'd woken up in the prison hospital.

It just happens that they had managed to prise the door open wide enough for a prison officer to squeeze through into the cell. He then managed to reach me before it was too late. I was later told that if it had been a few seconds longer it would've been too late. I was put on suicide watch for a while, but after about two weeks I was granted bail from the Judge in Chambers. I was released from prison and I soon forgot about what had happened and continued with life outside as normal, acting as though nothing had happened. The truth be known; I was bragging to all my friends about what it was like 'in the big house' (Strangeways Prison) and for a while I was walking around acting like a gangster. Obviously, I didn't mention about trying to commit suicide because I didn't want it to spoil my reputation.

*   *   *   *

16

THE LIKELY LADS

I was introduced to Rob and Harry who were both from Scotland. They were a pair of crafty thieves who travelled around the country looking for the opportunity to make easy money. They were involved in all kinds of criminal activities: smash 'n' grabs at jewellery stores and ram raids were their speciality. When I started to work with them I was making more money than I could count. I was still taking drugs at the time although I'd cut down on my drinking. My addiction to drugs was becoming more intolerable and I started to take big risks in what I was doing.

It was through these lads that I started to get involved with organised crime and it was during the summer of 1986 that a string of museums and stately homes were burgled throughout England, Scotland and Wales. Items such as gold, silver and jade were stolen and were immediately shipped out of the country to places like America and Germany. It was a busy year for us and we were making good money out of it all. The police didn't have a clue about the culprits until one day they had a real breakthrough.

Rob was visiting with some old friends and was having a friendly drink in the bar when the *Crime Watch* programme was showing a reconstruction of the burglaries on BBC1. He made a joke about the police not knowing where to look and he was overheard by somebody while he was boasting about the job. It just so happened that the person who heard him bragging was an off-duty police officer so it wasn't long before he was put under surveillance by the Serious Crime Squad in London. The surveillance went on for several months and during that time I was brought into the picture.

Besides grafting with the Scottish pair, I was also busy working by myself: committing burglaries and breaking into safes. My life was rather hectic by now and there didn't seem to be any end in sight. I wasn't aware that we were under surveillance as I continued to get involved deeper and deeper into a life of crime than I'd ever been before. I heard that Rob had been arrested for a robbery in Scotland and I lost contact with him for a while.

One night I went out with a friend and we made a beeline for the city centre of Manchester. It was easy pickings and we soon found ourselves jumping over a wall into the yard of a large loading bay for the Royal Mail. It was full of articulated lorries and it wasn't long before we were crashing through the gates with a fully loaded 40-foot-long Royal Mail lorry, stacked to the brim with thousands of parcels that were waiting to be delivered around the country. It was a good touch for us that evening and after unloading the stolen goods we decided to hit the town and celebrate our haul.

We were drinking right throughout the night and it while we were walking home in the early hours of the morning we noticed a window open on the second floor of a warehouse. Never ones to miss an opportunity, we climbed up the drainpipe and ended up breaking into the place. It was a busy night that night and we soon sobered up. After several visits to the warehouse, my house was packed to the brim with thousands of branded sports bags.

This cycle continued for several weeks until I received a call from a friend late one night. He was a good mate who I'd known for years and I knew that I could trust him. We arranged to get together to discuss ways of making money.

*   *   *   *

17

THE HOTEL ROBBERY

We arranged to meet at my house the following week. My neighbour at the time had approached me with a proposition to earn some quick and easy money. I turned her down at first and said that I wasn't interested, but curiosity got the better of me and I invited her over to hear what she had to say. It turned out that she had a grudge against her brother-in-law who owned a hotel in Crewe, Nantwich. She resented the fact that her sister was doing so well in life and wanted to teach her a lesson. I said that I'd think about it and sent her away.

A week later, while I had friends around at the house, the doorbell rang. I opened the door to find my neighbour. I invited her inside and introduced her to my friends. She provided us with information about the hotel and she insisted that the best time to rob the hotel was on a weekend while there was renovation work taking place on the main part of the building. It sounded like a walk in the park, so one weekend, we arranged a visit to the hotel as guests to see if the information was kosher.

There was indeed renovation work being done in the living quarters of the hotel and it was exactly where she said it was. After a few more careful checks and plans for the escape route we decided to do the job without any further delay. It was agreed the robbery should be carried out on the Friday night when the takings were expected to be as high as £100,000 in cash. Also, the information we had been given was that there was around £40,000 in jewellery, just sitting there waiting to be taken.

At 6.00pm on a Friday night I turned up at my mate's house. We went through the plan together one more time making sure that we didn't miss out on any of the details and that everybody knew their role for the job. We had the balaclavas and weapons all arranged and ready to go and spent the next half hour waiting for the car to come and pick us up. A blue BMW finally arrived with the getaway driver at the wheel. We set off from Manchester that night, singing and laughing away as though we were on a day trip going on a family picnic. Eventually, nearly an hour later, we drove into the car park of the hotel and, even though it was dark, we could see a lovely collection of cars parked up in the drive, ranging from BMWs, Mercedes and Bentleys, to silver and gold coloured Rolls Royce's. It reeked of money and it looked like we were going to make a good amount of cash that night.

We sat there and waited for a moment until, almost automatically, we all jumped out of the car and started running towards the hotel. It was like watching a scene from a Crime Watch programme, only this was the real McCoy. There was no turning back now: the robbery was something that had to be carried out regardless. I remember everything seemed to go into slow motion. Even though we had snorted enough cocaine between us that night to kill a herd of elephants, everybody appeared to be in control. We all knew our part and had no doubt about our roles to play in the robbery. It was a job well planned and thought through: it had taken two months of careful planning. I started to feel the adrenalin and drugs pumping through my body, which was a strong sensation, but it just added to the excitement and dangers of what was about to happen.

We could hear music coming through from the room downstairs which was the ballroom. We could tell it was packed with guests who were having a party as we heard the music and people talking, laughing and dancing. We heard all this when we barged into the hotel foyer with masks covering our faces and weapons drawn. We were tooled up to the eyeballs and ready for anything.

We started to run up the stairs making our way to the bedroom where the money was supposed to be stashed. Within seconds I could hear a crashing noise from another room. I thought that it was gun shots but realised later that one of the lads had burst into an office and was smashing through another door to break into the safe. At the same time, I charged into the main bedroom and was confronted by the hotel owner who was trying to get out of bed.

I was shouting like a demon-possessed man. I raised the sawn-off shotgun and pointed it in the direction of the hotel owner, threatening to blow his head off if he moved another inch. He realised that I was serious and remained perfectly still. After the introduction was over there wasn't another word said. I remember that there was a lot of shouting and banging going on in the other rooms. It sounded as though gun shots were being fired in every direction. I was fully aware that the alarm had already been raised and that other people in the hotel would be alerted to the noises that were coming from upstairs.

It seemed like an eternity, but it all happened within five minutes. There was a lot of confusion and I wasn't sure about what to do next. I decided to wait a while for the others to see what happened. Then my mate came running into the bedroom with a tray of money in large bundles of £50 notes. I was looking around to see if they had picked up the gold watches and chains we'd been told about but everything was moving so fast now it seemed the best thing to do was to clear off and escape while the going was good.

We started to make a dash for the main entrance when one of the lads decided that he wanted to take a detour. He made a run towards the ballroom where everybody had been earlier. He wanted to take guests' jewellery and money he even wanted to take some hostages for good measure. Thankfully that didn't happen which was just as well because we were rapidly running out of time. Instead we bolted towards the front door – which seemed a million miles away – but we just kept on running and finally we made it outside with only seconds to spare.

As the car skidded out of the car park we could hear the police sirens which weren't too far away and getting closer by the second. It sounded as though the whole of the Cheshire Constabulary was called out to deal with this one robbery. We carried on driving at high speeds through the country lanes, screeching around the tight corners without any thought or concern for oncoming traffic. It was a classic getaway and before long we found ourselves driving through the familiar streets of Manchester. Everybody was laughing and joking, and looking forward to counting out the money. It wasn't until we arrived back at the house did we realise that our haul didn't match up to our expectations. We came away with only £8,500 which was a real disappointment. And to add insult to injury the stash of gold that we had anticipated wasn't anywhere to be seen.

It wasn't until nine days later that we found out the awful truth of this blunder and kicked ourselves for overlooking this small mistake. Although the robbery was planned in a military fashion, we didn't realise that while the renovation of the hotel was taking place, the room where the money and gold were supposed to be stored was moved into an adjoining room for safe keeping while the builders completed their work. Even more haunting, was the news that armed police had been lying in wait for us at the hotel for two nights prior to the robbery taking place. They had received a tip-off that an armed gang was going to raid the hotel and the Serious Crime Squad officers from Manchester and Cheshire police were positioned inside and around the hotel waiting for us to turn up. After two days of surveillance and no sight of the robbers, the police had finally decided to call the whole thing off and left the hotel.

*   *   *   *

PART FOUR

18. ARRESTED FOR ROBBERY

I didn't go home for a couple of days after the robbery. I was too busy enjoying the night clubs in Manchester city centre with my friends. Unaware of anything suspicious, we were driving through the estate talking about the robbery and boasting about how it had been a good little earner. We were even discussing another job that was coming up soon, which would bring in enough money to see us through for a long time. I had to call at my house first to pick up a few clothes along with my passport. Nobody suspected anything unusual as we drove into the area where I lived and we weren't aware that the police had been tipped off about the robbery; they had been waiting at my house since it had happened.

We found out later that they had set up a special unit of surveillance teams and had been waiting for us to return to the house. I was in the car with three other people when we drove into the cul-de-sac where I lived. We were feeling too confident so were too high off our heads on drugs we notice nothing out of the ordinary. When the car came to a stop the area was practically deserted, which was very unusual because at that time of the day there would normally be a handful of kids and teenagers playing around outside the house . . . but there weren't any to be seen.

There was a window cleaner who I didn't recognise and a postman who was delivering letters on a Sunday morning (which was unheard of) who seemed stuck in transit. He wasn't moving at all but was looking over to the car when we pulled up outside. The police were taking no chances and it wasn't until we had all got out of the car and gone into the house that they made their move. It all happened so fast without any warning, armed police started to appear from every direction.

They'd been lying in wait, and while some were running from upstairs, others came crashing through the front and back doors shouting for us to freeze and stay where we were. I tried to escape but wherever I turned there were police who were built like brick houses blocking my way. It was a hopeless task and I realised that there was no way I was going to escape from them. I threw my hands in the air and gave myself up.

It all happened as fast as the robbery did, within minutes it was all over. Everybody was handcuffed and transported in separate cars to different police stations around the country. I was known by the police and, because I'd escaped from custody in times past, they were taking no chances. I was completely surrounded and was escorted by armed police along the motorway until we reached our destination which was thirty miles away. I was still not aware of what I'd been arrested for but I knew it wasn't for non-payment of fines – this was entirely different.

It was a grim sight when we arrived at the police station in Chester. There was an unsightly reception waiting for us as we walked in through the main entrance.

I knew that I couldn't fight my way through this and decided to keep schtum – at least until I found out what I'd been arrested for because I was still in the dark about this and I didn't have a clue.

After being booked-in at the reception I was placed in a cell for a while until they decided to come and visit. They came team-handed, escorted me upstairs where, for the first time, I finally found out the reason why I had been arrested. Even then I couldn't believe it was to do with the robbery.

The police seemed quite amused to have caught me off-guard and started the interview with real smug smiles on their faces. Throughout that first day of interviews, after many hours of interrogation I refused to answer any of their questions and demanded to have my solicitor present, but they refused my request and continued to pummel me with their many questions. At first, they had started the interviews with the softly-softly approach but, when they realised that they weren't getting anywhere with that, they applied a more forceful tactic by using threats, trying to intimidate me into making a statement.

I refused to take any further part in the interviews and adamantly refused to make any comments in response to their questions. My head was going around in circles wondering how on earth this had happened. My mind was totally battered through fatigue and at the same time my body was desperately craving another fix. They dropped the bombshell after the second day of interviews by showing me sworn statements from people that I knew, saying that I was there on the night of the robbery.

I knew that the evidence they had against me so far was all circumstantial, and what frustrated them most was that they knew that too. I was also aware that they were running out of time and sooner or later they were going to have to charge me with something or let me go. It was at this point that I decided I wasn't going to leave the cell without having my solicitor present during the interviews. It had been nearly three days and I'd still not been able to see my solicitor because they wouldn't oblige, so I stuck to my guns and refused to leave.

It was a stalemate and whenever they tried to take me out of the cell for questioning I would threaten to kick off and hurt as many police as possible. At first, they didn't take it seriously and tried to remove me from the cell heavy-handedly, I retaliated ferociously and fought with them tooth and nail. In the process, I managed to seriously assault two police officers. After that they left me alone for a while. It was like a battleground, I didn't care either way because I didn't have anything to lose.

I was finally allowed to see my solicitor and throughout the interviews, made no comments to their questioning. It came to the point where they had to make a decision, with what little evidence they had against me they decided to charge me with the robbery and with the assaults on the two police officers. It was the weekend, the courts were closed but an emergency hearing was held before the magistrates' courts in Crewe, Nantwich. It was a very short hearing and I was remanded in custody without bail to await trial at Risley Remand Centre in Warrington.

*   *   *   *

19

GRISLY RISLEY

Risley is located at an old army base near Warrington which is about twenty-two miles from Walton Prison in Liverpool. Over the years, it had earned its name of 'Grisly Risley' and was renowned for being one of the most violent prisons in the country. On the outside, it looked structurally sound but when you entered the prison itself you would see a whole new picture. I'd been charged for the robbery at the hotel and was committed to stand trial at Chester Crown Court and again refused bail. The prison itself was literally falling to pieces, when I had first arrived my immediate reaction was to ask for a transfer to Strangeways Prison which was a lot closer to home and was much easier for my family to visit.

The layout of the prison was similar to that of cell block H, but only on a much smaller scale. There were tiers which housed around sixty inmates on each level. It was very compact with hardly any room to manoeuvre. When I entered the cell for the first time I realised that it wasn't like the cells in a normal prison and I couldn't help but notice how small it was. My head was practically touching the ceiling. There were two buckets in the corner of the cell filled with urine and faeces. The stench was so overpowering that it made me feel like I wanted to vomit and I could hardly breathe. My attention was drawn to the walls of the cell, I noticed writing on the wall that was painted in blood-red letters about twenty-inches high and were sketched around the cell saying, 'WELCOME TO THE PLEASURE DOME!' That was really freaky, so were the pictures of Pink Floyd that were painted all over the walls and ceiling too.

It felt as though I'd walked through a time zone and had stepped into another world. The prison was overpopulated with inmates, mainly Scousers from Liverpool and Birkenhead. I realised when I arrived that there were only a handful of Mancunians who were outnumbered by the Liverpudlians by about 50 to 1. Due to the lousy conditions and the prison being so overcrowded there was a tense atmosphere between the inmates and the prison guards who were desperately trying to maintain control of the prison.

Fighting was an everyday occurrence at Risley and it was mainly about drugs and money. When I first arrived, I was on my own, but managed to meet up with my co-accused who was already at the prison. We were separated into different cells, but we soon managed to swing it with the screws to allow us to be padded up in the same cell together. We were all packed with enough drugs to last us for a while and, within hours of us settling down in our cell, we were selling cannabis and amphetamines around the wings.

Risley wasn't anything like the other prisons that I'd been to before. Unlike Strangeways Prison with its strict regime there didn't seem to be any law and order in this place. The inmates had control of the running of the whole prison. It was as though the lunatics were running the asylum. It housed a variety of people from all walks of life but consisted of mainly speed freaks, smack-heads and dope pushers. Not to forget the cockroaches which outnumbered the inmates by about 100 to 1 – and that's without any exaggerating!

There were no toilet facilities in the cells or any running water which made the conditions absolutely appalling. Everything seemed to revolve around drugs and violence. There was always some sort of conflict between the inmates and the screws on a daily basis. The food wasn't fit for human consumption. I remember queuing up for my meal on the first day and an inmate was standing in the line complaining bitterly about the state of the food. I watched as the screws laughed and told him to shut up however, when the inmate was served his food he turned around with the metal tray in his hands and smashed it sideways into one of the screws face and told him to eat it himself. There was a really bad atmosphere in the place where you constantly had to watch your back.

A PP9 (which is a 9-volt battery that was used to power radios) were tucked away into some socks and was considered a favourite tool for the Scousers. Along with the heads of razor blades which were melted into the end of toothbrush handles and regularly used as a weapon such was the madness of the place. It was their way of dishing out punishment and also dealing with an argument. I remember thinking to myself when I first arrived that whoever had designed this prison must've been on drugs himself. It definitely wasn't built for the rehabilitation of inmates and there was nothing to suggest anything other than it being a holding centre to house the criminally insane.

After spending several weeks on remand and travelling to and from the magistrates courts every week, all our efforts for getting bail were exhausted. It was left to the Judge in Chambers to decide whether or not bail should be considered, but that was going to be a long process. So, in the meantime, we knuckled down and started to settle into everyday life inside prison. I had regular visits from my family and friends. And on occasions my friends would smuggle drugs into the prison. I looked forward to these visits because they would keep us up to date with everything that was happening in the outside world. Also, they would bring us plenty of food and drink, along with a change of clothes.

In the meantime, every effort was being made to prevent the prosecution witnesses from coming to court and giving evidence. They were being threatened and sometimes violence was used to intimidate them to change their statements. In some cases, witnesses were offered a bribe to stay away from court on the day of the trial. The main prosecution witness, who was a real threat to our defence, even had a contract put out on her life. She was on 24-hour police protection over the following months and was secretly moved to different locations around the Manchester area for her own safety. It seemed that no matter what we did to stop any of the witnesses from turning up at court and giving evidence it wasn't working it just made matters about a million times worse for us.

We spent twelve months on remand at Risley waiting for the trial to start for the robbery. The evidence against my co-accused was overwhelming. When they were arrested, they were found with balaclavas, masks, photos of the hotel, guns, and even money taken from the hotel. The Crown Prosecution's case was strongly against them, it more or less secured a guaranteed conviction twelve months later. It was different with the evidence against me which was non-existent. I wasn't found with anything to incriminate myself in that robbery, or any other robbery for that matter. Apart from a couple of witness statements the evidence against me was all circumstantial and it was very likely that I would be walking away scot-free on the first day of the trial.

While I was awaiting trial on the robbery charge I received visits from Serious Crime Squad officers from all over the country who were investigating a spate of burglaries which had been committed on museums and stately homes throughout England, Scotland and Wales. Obviously, I denied any involvement in this and managed to keep them away for a while. However, while I was still on remand they were busy gathering evidence from other sources, it was a few months later that I was finally charged with conspiracy to steal £250,000 from the stately home. At that time, there was a public outcry because the many items that were stolen were family heirlooms and it was very unlikely that any of the stolen goods were ever going to be recovered.

*   *   *   *

20

THE ROBBERY TRIAL

It was raining and the traffic through to Chester was abysmal. We were being transported to the Crown Court in Chester to stand trial for robbery. There was a strange silence and feeling of apprehension in the air between us and nobody wanted to talk. We had waited twelve months for the trial to get started and now it was time to face the music. The previous night we were discussing the trial together and I was left thinking about what I was going to do when I was released. I was planning on shooting dead three of the main prosecution witnesses for making statements against us and for coming to court to swear our lives away. It didn't cross my mind that I was as guilty as hell. I just wanted to see the criminal code of justice carried out and, regardless of the consequences, I was going to carry my threat out to the letter.

The prison bus had finally arrived and we were quickly escorted to the cells which were directly underneath the courts. It was while we were waiting for the trial to start that something extraordinary happened in the cell which would shake me to the core. I just want to say at this stage that it was totally unexpected from my part and it was an experience that I had never anticipated. So, when it did happen, nobody was more surprised than I was because I believe from that moment it was the turning point in my life. It was an event that changed everything and, looking back now, I realise it had saved three innocent people from being killed.

I was sitting in the cells while I was waiting to go into the courts and was in discussion with my co-accused about the trial ahead of us. I wasn't too bothered as I knew that I had a very strong chance of walking out with a 'not guilty' verdict. There was even talk that the charges against me would be dropped before the trial even started. I stopped talking for a while and was reflecting on what was being discussed that morning when suddenly something happened. It was weird because everything in the cell seemed to go deadly silent where I couldn't even hear myself breathe. It was as though I was being elevated into another room with nothing but total silence all around.

Suddenly, I heard a voice that was saying, 'John, I want you to plead "guilty" today.' It was crystal clear and it felt as though somebody was standing behind me. I turned around quickly and immediately thought that it was one of my mates having a laugh. when I looked around to see which one was playing the joke, I realised that they were both engrossed in conversation at the other end of the cell. I thought to myself that I must've been hearing things, and tried to shake the thought out of my mind. Again, I heard the same voice, this time it was with more urgency and was saying, 'John, I want you to plead guilty today, not only to make yourself right with the courts but also to put things right with God!'

I couldn't believe what I was hearing and thought

that I was going crazy. It went against everything that I believed in however, I had an awful feeling inside that if I didn't listen to this voice that something dreadful was going to happen in my life. I knew from deep within my heart that I couldn't argue my case and I had to obey this voice. I turned to my friends and told them that I was changing my plea from 'not guilty' to 'guilty'. They couldn't believe it and tried to persuade me to change my mind, but I'd already decided what I was going to do and I wasn't going to be swayed from making this decision.

I called my barrister downstairs from the courtroom and told him of my intentions. He also tried to persuade me to change my mind and even threatened that if I pleaded guilty he would refuse to represent me. He tried to explain the consequences of what would happen if I continued to go through with it but it didn't matter what he said, because I was adamant that I was doing the right thing. I told him, that even if it meant that I was going into the courts without legal representation, I was going to plead guilty regardless of what he said.

There was a real urgency in my spirit with what I was doing and even though I understood it went against the grain and the criminal code of conduct, it didn't matter. It wasn't that important to me anymore. So, it was against everybody's pleas and arguments that I boldly walked into the courts that morning and changed my plea to 'guilty'. The courts accepted my plea and I was sent back to Walton Prison to await sentencing. I cannot explain what I was thinking at that time but there was a real sense of peace around me. It's difficult to describe the way that I was feeling, for the first time in my life, I felt good inside. I also knew that I would be receiving a hefty prison sentence, but that didn't matter because I knew that I'd made the right decision.

It wasn't until the next day that I realised what had happened. Suddenly I came to my senses – but it was too late. The damage had already been done and there was nothing that I could do to reverse the situation. I'd pleaded guilty at the trial and it's because of this decision that I had sealed my own fate. I wasn't happy about the prospect of serving several years in prison and I made another decision: I would try and escape at the first opportunity. My mates both went through with the trial and, half way through, one of them decided to change his plea to guilty because the case was seriously going against him. The other continued through to the end of the trial and, not surprisingly, he was found guilty.

*   *   *   *

PART FIVE

21. WALTON PRISON

In October 1987 I received my first prison sentence. The judge had branded me a menace to society and he wasn't hesitant in sentencing me to seven years' imprisonment. I can't remember much about it because I was stoned out of my head at the time he was passing sentence. I was told later that I'd received eleven years for the robbery which was then reduced to seven years because I'd pleaded guilty before the trial had started. After the judge, had finished with his sentencing, he ordered that we be taken down to the cells. I was finally a convicted prisoner and was informed that we wouldn't be returning to Risley that day but that we would be transported from the courts straight on through to Walton Prison in Liverpool.

I'd already been involved in many fights with the Scousers while I was on remand at Risley and now that I was at Walton Prison I found myself in the very heart of Liverpool. I anticipated more trouble ahead and it was with this attitude that I arrived at Walton with all guns blazing. I was determined in my mind that I wouldn't be taking any trouble from anybody. I was allocated a job in the mailbag section of the prison and it wasn't long before I was involved in my first fight. I wasn't looking for trouble but when it came I couldn't avoid it. I was working on a sewing machine when some inmate approached me and made a comment that I didn't hear at the time. I decided to ignore it but I could feel there was tension in the air about something and wasn't sure what it was about.

Another inmate later told me about what had happened in the workshop. He warned me that one of the inmates was looking for trouble and had passed the word around that he was going to knife me at the first opportunity. I was new to the prison and I knew that I had to 'set my bones' – give an example to everybody – to show that I wasn't to be messed around with. I sat through the night thinking about this and wondered what to do about the situation. I knew that I couldn't back down because this would make my life hell. So, I decided to bide my time and strike at the first opportunity.

The next day I was in the workplace and sitting down doing some work. I was sewing the mailbags together using a large pair of shears when I sensed the atmosphere in the place had changed.

There were civilian staff working in the mailbag room milling around at the time, but they weren't aware of what was about to happen. When I looked up from where I was working I also realised that the screws had sensed that something was about to happen and had conveniently disappeared from sight. I remember the usual loud noise of inmates talking and the radio that was blaring away, had somehow faded into the background. The stage had been set and it seemed as though all eyes were on me. I thought to myself that this was it and I knew that I had to prove myself to everybody. I didn't care what crime the other inmate was inside for, and it didn't matter to me how big or hard he was, I just knew that I had to put him down on the floor regardless.

There was a toilet reception area in the workplace where the inmates would go for a smoke and a break. The other inmate was already inside and he was waiting for me to join him. It was like clockwork when I stood to my feet and walked towards where he was standing. Inside prison, 60 per cent of the time the threats that are made by inmates aren't really carried out, and the majority of inmates are just as nervous as each other. This occasion however, I took his threat very seriously. When I walked into the reception area I knew that there was only going to be one outcome. A prison guard was using the toilet when I walked inside; he realised what was about to happen next and made a quick run for the exit.

Without any warning or hesitation, I launched myself into an atrocious attack on the inmate, completely taking my opponent off guard. It seemed as though I was taking all my frustrations over the years out on him. Before he knew what was happening, he was lying on the floor unconscious and covered in blood. I continued to kick and punch him until there was no movement in his body. The alarm had been raised and within minutes there were around ten prison guards standing only yards away from where I was. They were shouting for me to stop and were afraid to come any closer because of the amount of blood that was spread around the floor. They thought that I had used the mail bag shears to stab the inmate and that I still had the weapon in my hands.

I suddenly stopped and turned towards the screws, reassuring them it was all over. I repeatedly reassured them that no weapons had been used and before I knew what was happening I was overpowered and taken down into the punishment cells.

This was my first introduction to Walton Prison. I'd been there for less than a week and already fighting for survival. After what had happened in this incident nobody bothered me. I spent a week in the block (punishment cell) and when I came out I was treated like a hero. The other guy was transferred to another prison for his own safety and I never saw him again – which was great because I didn't want any reprisals.

*   *   *   *

22

ATTEMPTED ESCAPE

While I was on remand for the robbery, I was charged with conspiracy to commit the burglaries on the museums and stately homes. It was quite serious and my barrister had tried to get the charges included with the robbery charge, but the Crown Prosecution Service wasn't having any of it and managed to keep the charges from coming together. A week after I'd been sentenced for the robbery at Chester Crown Court I was transported by taxi to the Huddersfield magistrates' courts to answer to the conspiracy and burglary charges. I was escorted by two prison officers who had warned me before leaving Walton that I'd better not try to escape.

I was still quite livid about being sentenced to seven years and was secretly scheming to escape. I thought that it was a great opportunity when I arrived at the courts and, after being signed over from the prison authorities into the custody of local 'jam-jams' (court officials), I knew that it was just a matter of time and I'd be free. When I arrived at the courts I quickly realised that there was very little security around and that it wouldn't be too difficult. I noticed every little nook and cranny about the holding area where I was being moved to. I even noticed the way out, but I didn't let my sudden interest in the courts' new security system draw the attention of my guards. I acted like the model prisoner and this helped ease the tension a little because they had been warned that I might try and escape.

It was lunchtime and most of the guards had gone away for their dinner. I was packed into a cell along with around four other prisoners who were waiting for their court appearances. I took advantage of this and made my move. I started stuffing loads of newspapers down the toilet in the cell and, after flushing it a few times, the whole area was flooded. When the security guard came around he noticed the water pouring out of the cell and he made the mistake of opening the door that was it. The opportunity to escape came far too easily, before he realised what was happening, he was dragged into the cell where I managed to grab the keys from him.

He tried to put up a fight, but it was like wrestling with a rabid dog. There was no way that I was going back to prison now, and I wasn't going to let him stop me from escaping. I ended up locking him in a cell and started to run towards the exit. I heard the guard was shouting and banging on the cell door, I didn't care about that. I knew that freedom was only seconds away and while I was still holding the keys to the outside world I thought to myself that nobody was ever going to stop me from getting out of that place.

While I was rushing around I was trying to remember the way out, for a split second, my mind became confused. I had to stop and think about where the exit was and then it happened again. It was as though I was blinded temporarily because of a great white light suddenly flashed before me, I heard that same voice that

I'd heard previously. It said, 'Drop the keys on the floor,' but I refused to listen and continued running. The keys started to heat up in my hands which became unbearably hot, without thinking any further, I obeyed the voice and released the keys from my hand. It had all happened in a split second. Although I was still confused I continued to run towards the exit with my heart nearly beating through my chest.

I was determined to escape and was desperately looking for the nearest exit. But it was a hopeless task because while I was running around like a headless chicken the sirens were blasting throughout the whole building. I could hear shouting coming from almost every direction and I could also hear heavy boots stomping around the corner. My heart started to sink as I realised that I was surrounded by security guards and prison officers who had been alerted to what was happening. When I realised that I wasn't going to escape I stopped running. I turned around and found myself faced with around a dozen angry men. They were making their way towards me slowly with their truncheons drawn. At that point I knew that the game was up . . . and I was in for a good kicking!

I had nothing to lose and like a suicide bomber on a mission I just ran towards them, fighting like a mad maniac. I was outnumbered and was soon handcuffed with my hands behind my back; my feet were also cuffed to prevent any further attempts to break free. I was whisked in and out of the magistrates' court with a heavy escort and a few red faces. When the magistrates were informed about what had happened they rushed through with the preliminaries and another hearing was set for a later date. It wasn't long before I was making my way back to the prison in a police van. I wasn't too bothered about receiving a beating because at that time I was more concerned about what had happened in the courts when I tried to escape.

I was mystified by what I'd heard and experienced and, even though I was still feeling confused, I could clearly remember hearing that voice and I wondered to myself what on earth it was all about. Instead of travelling by taxi I was thrown into a police van which had two coppers inside. The screws who had escorted me to the courts were in the front with the driver. Although I was still handcuffed with my hands behind my back, I managed to get into a fight with the police escorts in the back of the vehicle. I was already battered and bruised from the beating that I'd received after trying to escape and I knew that there wasn't going to be a warm reception when I returned to the prison – so I just exploded and head-butted the closest copper without warning. I remember his partner launching himself across the van trying to pin me down on the floor. I just snapped and in the process managed to break free from my handcuffs.

At the same time, there were three other prisoners who were also being transported to the prison. While I was wrestling with the police they, too, started to join in with the fight. It was total chaos and I can remember the van was rocking from side to side for a good number of miles on the motorway. I was finally overpowered and handcuffed again, but I continued spitting, kicking and biting at every opportunity. The last thing that I could remember was laughing like a madman. It was against the law to stop on the motorway and open a vehicle transporting prisoners from the courts to the prison. I did everything that I could to make their journey as uncomfortable as possible. The van was speeding along the motorway and when we arrived at the prison the sirens were still blaring away. It didn't matter to me because when the doors were finally opened I was already knocked unconscious.

I was rushed straight through into the prison and was literally thrown into the punishment block. I was brought before the governor the next day and told that I'd be placed in patches until all the charges that I faced had been dealt with by the courts. As a category, E/A prisoner I was classed as a top security inmate and was segregated from the main part of the prison. I was allocated a cell on my own and made to wear a prison uniform with a yellow stripe ('patches') running down the front and back of my jeans and jacket, distinguishing me from any of the other prisoners in case I tried to escape. Wherever I went within the prison I was always escorted by at least two guards.

I picked up two more serious assault charges for the attack on the police who must've thought I was a complete lunatic.

*   *   *   *

23

ESCAPE TO REALITY

One day a prison officer threw a book called *Escape to Reality* into my cell. It was written by this guy called Tony Ralls. I wasn't really into reading books but this one sounded different. I flicked through the comments at the back and was quite interested to read about how Tony had escaped from living a life of crime and drug addiction. It was difficult to believe, I thought the book would make an interesting read so I decided to sit down and read it through anyway.

Tony was an ex-drug addict and had a criminal record like mine. I could relate to most of the stuff that he was talking about and it wasn't long before I found myself engrossed in reading his story. I identified with my own experiences of crime, drugs and prison, but it wasn't until I was half way through reading his book that the story began to change. He started rapping on about Jesus. He was writing about how he had had a spiritual experience with God whilst he was serving a prison sentence, how it had changed his life around for the better. I started to lose interest when he mentioned about God and I decided enough was enough.

I threw the book into the corner of the cell and gave it no more thought until a few days later. It had been an extremely long day and after writing all my letters and doing some work on my defence for my next trial,

I found that I had nothing else to do with my time. Almost immediately I felt something inside me that said, 'Why not pick the book up again, and this time read it with an open mind.' I thought about this and didn't see any harm in it. So, that's what I did – I picked the book up and decided to read it again.

I finally read the book from cover to cover (with an open mind!) and when I had finished reading it, I found that it was a powerful story. I wondered to myself whether or not to believe that his life had truly been completely transformed. At this stage I was struggling to think it was believable because it was such a fantastic story and was so incredulous. It seemed inconceivable to believe that God could transform somebody's life in such a dramatic way. And, although I had my doubts about it at the beginning, I secretly wanted it to be true.

Reading *Escape to Reality* made me look at my own life and question whether God really did exist. I knew that I had made a complete mess of my life and I only had myself to blame for that. Living a life of crime was the path that I chose from a very early age and I could never point the finger at anybody else for my being the way that I was. I always believed that I was a likeable person but, the more I thought about it, the more I realised how far from the truth that was. I started to see myself in a different light and realised how deceitful and conceited I'd become. It was quite a revelation when I also realised that I was selfish and self-centred, that I didn't care about anybody else but myself.

I believe from that moment I went on a journey of

self-discovery, the more that I delved into my past life the more I realised what a complete and utter failure I'd become. It was like looking into a mirror and seeing yourself for the first time. The more that I looked into the mirror, the more I realised that I didn't like the person I'd become. It's a true saying that 'you reap what you sow', and that's exactly what I was doing. I was reaping what I'd sown over the years when I was living a life of crime and constant drug abuse. I was paying the price for the crimes that I'd committed and the many people that I'd hurt along the way.

Although I'd been heavily addicted to drugs I was living a total and utter lie that everything was going to get better with my life. The reality was that it never did. I was on that slippery slope from the moment I put that first needle into my veins and when I decided to commit my first crime. I knew that I had to change somehow; otherwise I'd end up being found dead in some gutter one day or would most probably be serving a life sentence inside prison.

It was through reading the book *Escape to Reality* that, basically, pointed me in the right direction. I wanted to know whether it was true about God. I asked myself, *'If God was real then what would He think about me and my life?'* It's true when they say a leopard never changes its spots, but I wasn't a leopard and I wanted to know whether God could really change my life around. I didn't know how He was going to achieve this, but I just felt it in my spirit that I had to find out. And I knew that I should start this journey by going to church.

I must point out at this stage that my history of going to church was practically non-existent. Although my parents were both strong believing Catholics, their faith didn't really go any further than attending the occasional wedding, baptism or funeral. So, although I was born into a Roman Catholic background, I had no faith in God whatsoever and none of this meant zilch. When I was a young lad, I never actually went inside the church to hear what the preacher was saying. Instead, I was busy stealing the lead off the roof or was breaking into the cars parked outside on a Sunday with my mates. I didn't know anything about other denominations and, as far as I was concerned, there was only one church in existence and that was the Roman Catholic Church. I applied to the governor at Walton Prison to attend the Catholic service that Sunday morning.

I didn't know what to expect when I walked into the church, but I was on a mission and I just had to find out the truth. I was escorted into the chapel by two screws and an Alsatian dog. We were sat at the back of the church when the service started. I noticed that there were around a hundred inmates already in attendance and I thought to myself, 'Well this looks interesting,' and focused on what was going on with the inmates. In prison, inmates attend church for all different reasons. Some would go there because it breaks up the monotony of the day, whilst others would use it as an opportunity to meet up with their friends who they'd not seen for a while because they may be placed in a different part of the prison; this would be the only chance for them to get together and to catch up on old news. There were the genuine ones who went to church to find out more about God but there weren't many of those if the truth be told.

Then there was the type who would only attend if they thought that it would help with their chances of receiving an early release from prison on parole. It was comical in a round-about way, because these inmates were obvious and easy to identify. You would often see them walking around the prison with a crucifix around their neck or even a set of rosary beads, which was the joke of the century. 'Well, each to their own,' I thought. When the service was finished, they would sink back into their cell smoking pot and the usual garb that goes with it.

It was a traditional Catholic service where the priest would come out dressed in his robes with his little entourage waving the incense around the place. I noticed that hardly anybody was taking a blind bit of notice at this stage. They seemed more interested in talking amongst themselves than paying any attention to what was happening.

Tobacco, drugs and money was exchanging hands while the priest was doing his usual bit. I could see everything from where I was sitting. Prison guards were spread around the chapel but they seemed oblivious to what was going on. After a while, the priest started the service by asking everybody to join together in singing the first song. It was hilarious almost like clockwork mice, they started singing in unison; a few inmates even started clapping, which I thought was so ridiculous and false. I felt like laughing out loud, and nearly did, but thought better of it.

I was starting to get extremely bored and wanted to leave before the service had finished, but I remembered the reason why I was there and thought to myself, 'If God is real then surely I will meet Him in this place.' There was no chance of that happening because I watched, and waited, and even tried to listen for God to turn up, but it seemed that God was as far and distant as my release date. I came out of the meeting feeling rather disappointed but, while I was being escorted out of the church, I managed to 'half-inch' (steal) a small Bible which I stuck down the front of my trousers.

It wasn't until I arrived back at my cell that I realised the full impact of what I'd done. I'm sure that if I'd asked the priest for a copy then he wouldn't have minded giving me a Bible – but why break a habit of a lifetime? I thought to myself that it wasn't the time to develop a conscience just yet. So, when I finally arrived back at my cell, and the door was shut behind me, I sat down at the end of the bed and looked at the New Testament Bible for the first time in my life. It was a strange feeling but it felt as though I was being watched and I can remember how quiet it was all around me in that solitary cell. I didn't waste any more time, before I knew what was happening, I found myself sitting down and reading the Bible from cover to cover.

Wow, did that really happen? Never in a million years would anybody believe that I'd just spent the last two days reading the word of God. When I finished reading the book of Revelation – it's the last book of the Bible – I felt as though I'd just had a personal revelation and insight into another world. The truth of God's word hit me right between the eyes. I was not only faced with the truth but I knew in my heart that I had to make a decision. I closed the Bible, shut my eyes, and suddenly I heard a still quiet voice that was speaking to me. It was asking, 'Do you believe it?' I didn't know that God could speak to you in this way and I didn't really know much about God for that matter (only what I'd read about Him). At that moment though I did know and realised that it was a calm and reassuring voice.

I recalled when I was in the courts while waiting for the trial for the robbery to start, I realised that it was the same voice that had spoken to me then. Without really thinking about anything else, I replied, 'YES, I DO BELIEVE!' Although I didn't understand everything that I'd just read, I knew just without a doubt that the story about Jesus was true. I wasn't sure what to do next. I didn't want to go back to the Catholic church as I had mixed feelings about the whole set-up. I couldn't hack the traditional bit and it had seemed so false and hypocritical. I felt very uncomfortable about the relics which were hanging on the walls, there was just something about it which didn't sit right with me. I decided that I wouldn't be going to that church again, I thought I would feel better to stay in solitude where I could sit and read the Bible without any distractions or the chance of being interrupted by anybody.

It wasn't until about two weeks later that I felt the need to attend church again. I was being escorted onto the exercise yard when I heard singing coming from the other side of the prison. I had to check myself because it sounded like angels singing. I turned to the screws and asked them, 'What's that all about?' and I remember one of them saying, 'You wouldn't be interested in any of those people because they're the born-again Christians.' Immediately alarm bells rang inside of me, I recalled that I'd read in the Bible about the early Christian Church and I just felt in my spirit that I had to find out for myself no matter what they said. I asked if I could see what it was all about, but the guards argued the point by saying that they couldn't change the programme. I was scheduled to go outside for an hour of exercise and they were adamant that the routine wasn't going to be broken.

I prayed a little prayer under my breath and asked God to help me into that meeting. It was a miracle in itself because without any further ado I found myself being escorted towards where the singing was coming from. I didn't have a clue what to expect but somehow, I just knew that I had to be there. I couldn't believe it when we walked up the landing and into what appeared to be someone's prison cell. I soon realised that it was an entrance into a small chapel which was converted by knocking the walls down from several prison cells. When we walked through into the chapel I soon realised that this was very different to the Catholic chapel that I had attended previously. I looked around when I walked through the door and I noticed that there were around forty inmates who were stood to their feet and singing aloud with their hands in the air. It was a good atmosphere all round and I felt myself wondering what on earth was going to happen next.

I sat at the back of the chapel along with both my guards and waited for the singing to subside not knowing what to expect. After a while the singing finally stopped and everybody started to sit down. It went quiet for a while and it was one of those moments where you could almost hear a pin drop. I couldn't believe it when this preacher stood up and started to speak about God. His appearance wasn't much to look at but it was the authority with which he spoke that grabbed my immediate attention. Is name being Malcolm Carter who was a Methodist minister (which was something that I found out later), but the most striking thing about him was that he didn't wear any fancy clothes, no dog-collar, nothing that smacked of religion.

I was thinking to myself at that time, 'What a difference from the old priest in the last place; maybe this guy's worth listening to.' Smack, bang, wallop, I'd never heard anything like it in my life. This small skinny preacher was speaking about God as though he knew him personally. I never realised that the reality of God's love could be explained in such a simple way. He left no stone unturned and preached the word of God with such a strong conviction that, before I knew what was happening, I wanted to respond to what he was saying. He talked about sin which separated us from God and the forgiveness of sin through what Jesus did on the cross. I felt convicted about what I was hearing and I found myself being challenged about making myself right with God. I didn't know how to go about this and I remember that I tried to get this man's attention by looking directly into his eyes. My thoughts were racing around in my head and all different kinds of questions were going through my mind.

I was thinking to myself, 'What is it that this man has got in his life? I want it!' I couldn't figure it out until suddenly there appeared around him a glow of light which was so obvious that I had to pinch myself to see if I was actually dreaming or imagining it. I even checked my guards who were sitting on either side of me to see if they could see what I was seeing. They were just sitting there with bored expressions on their faces. When I turned to look back at the preacher I could still see this amazing light around him. While he was speaking, I heard that same small reassuring voice saying, 'This man belongs to Me, and NOTHING in this world can touch him.'

I knew that voice, and this time it sounded much stronger and was spoken in a very assertive and authoritative manner. I actually thought that one of my guards was playing tricks, but when I looked in their direction I realised that they hadn't said anything – the first guard was paying more attention to his dog and was ruffling up its fur, while the second guard was turned in the other direction and was reading a small book. I couldn't figure it out at all until I suddenly realised that it was God who was speaking to me and was assuring me of His presence in the room. My head was whirling around. I was just about to jump up and shout out something when the speaker announced that the meeting had now ended. I realised that the screws had already stood up to leave and were already making their way to the door.

When I arrived back at my cell I paced the floor, thinking to myself, 'I must meet this man and speak with him.' I didn't even know his name. Suddenly I realised that something was happing I heard the rattling of keys and the door of my cell was being opened. A guard was standing there with this little preacher behind him. I invited him to come inside the cell, then the screw left us alone together he simply said, 'My name's Malcolm, and I'm a Methodist minister. I've come to speak with you and to tell you that God loves you, not only does God love you, but today God wants to SET YOU FREE!'

You could've knocked me over with a feather. I couldn't believe it when only moments earlier I was thinking about this man, now all of a sudden, he was standing there right in front of me! All my life I'd been suspicious of everybody and I'd never trusted anyone. Even though I loved my parents and family I would never allow them close enough to confide in them fully about what was going on in my life. Now here I was faced with a complete stranger whom I'd never met before but, for some reason, I felt that I could trust him with my life. It was a strange feeling one which I'd never experienced before. Without waiting a moment longer, I invited Malcolm to sit down and, for the next hour that he spent in that cell, I poured out my life story to him.

I related the story about how I had ended up inside and about how I had turned to crime and drugs at a very early age. I told him things that I never thought I'd ever share with anybody else in this life time. I seemed to be talking forever and it didn't matter what I said because I knew that this man wasn't standing over me in judgement. He sat and listened while I poured my heart out in that solitary cell. I told him that I wasn't happy about my life and that I'd done some terrible stuff that I wasn't proud of. I admitted that I'd made a complete mess of things and I knew all too well that I couldn't change myself and, for the life of me, I couldn't seem to put things right. I told him that I needed a miracle, but I didn't know what to do.

My addiction to drugs had taken its toll on my life through the ten years of constant drug abuse. It had destroyed my youth and I believe had taken the very life substance out of me. I admitted that I wasn't living anymore but that I was just surviving in this world. The drugs had affected me in every way, shape and form. The abuse had destroyed me in so many different ways: mentally, physically and psychologically. It was a real shambles and I knew it. I told him that I was genuinely fed up and tired of living like a zombie and I wanted to break free from this lifestyle, but I didn't know how. I told him that everybody I knew was involved with crime and drugs in some form or another. It had become a way of life for me and I just didn't know any other way.

But then Malcolm started to explain what the Bible says, about Jesus being the right way forward. I sat and I listened intently and then I started to cry. I knew while he speaking that he was telling the truth and I couldn't help but think to myself, 'But I've done some wicked things in my life,' and it was while I was thinking about this that I felt a real conviction come upon me. It wasn't just for the things that I was already inside for but I started feeling guilty about all the other stuff that I did throughout my life and hadn't been caught for. Surely, I thought to myself, God can't forgive me for everything. I was actually thinking about this when Malcolm started talking about God's forgiveness and he mentioned about Jesus dying for us on the cross and the sacrifice that he made on our behalf covered 'all our sins'!

It meant that if we confessed our sins before God and asked for His forgiveness, then we could have a clean slate. He would not only forgive us for everything that we've done in the past, but He has promised through His word that He will never raise the matter again.

I couldn't hold back any longer and I realised that I desperately wanted to get my life back together, and especially realised that I needed to make things right with God. When I look back over the years I can honestly say that my life was like somebody had been driving through the city centre in a ten-ton truck and was mowing everybody down without looking back. I asked Malcolm what to do next and very simply he said that I should say that I was sorry to God and then I should 'receive His forgiveness' for absolutely everything that I'd done in the past.

I didn't know how to pray but Malcolm said a prayer on my behalf and he explained that the word 'Amen'

111 ·

simply means 'that's my prayer too, so let it happen'. The prayer that he prayed was a simple prayer, but it was also very meaningful because that's what I wanted to happen. It went something like this:

Dear Lord Jesus, I've heard about what you did on the cross for me. I realise that it was a big commitment on Your part because I personally don't know anyone that would die for me. I acknowledge that 'I AM A SINNER' and the sin in my life separates me from Your Father in heaven. I come to You today and admit that I've got things wrong in my life. I need Your help, Lord Jesus, so please forgive me and help me to get my life together. I need You to help me to change in my attitude and behaviour because I know that without your help my life will be the same. Thank you, Lord Jesus, for loving me enough to die for my sins so that I can have eternal life. Amen!

I said, 'Amen' to the prayer and I meant every word of it because I said it straight from my heart. I then added my own bit at the end which was, 'God, if You are real, then please come and live in my heart, and if you can do anything with this messed up life of mine I promise that I will follow You and will serve You until I take my final breath.' That was my prayer and hopefully that will be yours too. I know without a doubt that if you've said this prayer for yourself and have been sincere in your heart when you prayed it, then God WILL FORGIVE YOU! I didn't expect angels to appear when I was praying but I did feel at total peace with myself when I had finished.

*'But with you there is forgiveness, so that we can,
with reverence, serve you.'* Psalm130:4

It was amazing what happened next because within a
very short period I realised that I'd started to change
inside. It was a matter of days when I thought that I'd do
a little assessment of my life and see what had happened
since making that simple prayer. I realised that I'd
stopped swearing completely and I know that some
people would be thinking, 'Well, what's the big deal
about that?' But it meant so much to me because all
throughout my life I was used to swearing like a trooper
and it had become like a second language to me.
I couldn't have a conversation with anybody without
swearing every other word. I also noticed that there was
a dramatic change in my attitude towards other people,
especially with the screws who I had a real hate
relationship with – but even this started to change.

I started to see things differently and I started to
view life from a whole new perspective. I realised that
the screws were normal human beings with families of
their own who were paid to keep lunatics like me off the
streets. Instead of looking for any opportunity to pick a
fight with them, I started to say 'hello' and 'good morning'
to my guards. It was incredible – but true. When I first
came into prison I was constantly fighting and arguing
with the screws, also with the inmates. I knew a lot of
people inside prison and I had a reputation to live up to,
but that didn't seem to matter anymore because I didn't
care about my reputation. It was as though I'd been
liberated from the responsibility of having to live up to
other people's expectations.

'Therefore, if anyone is in Christ, the new creation has come: the old has gone, the new is here!' 2 Corinthians 5:17

I know that there have been thousands of prisoners who have been through the British penal system over the years, and the majority of those have battled against the system hoping to get one over on the authorities. Like the many thousands before me, I was one of those people who were too stupid to realise that I was fighting a losing battle. My attitude started to change dramatically and I'm just glad that I realised this sooner rather than later. I realised that I wasn't angry anymore and, rather than looking for trouble, it seemed that I became the peacemaker instead. I felt really good inside and although I'd been hammered with years in prison by the courts, I'd never felt better in all my life.

*   *   *   *

24

THE CONSPIRACY TRIAL

Nineteen months after I'd been sentenced to seven years for the robbery I was moved to Armley Prison in Leeds to stand trial for the conspiracy charge. It was while I was there that I met up with Rob and Harry who had been held on remand at Barlinnie Prison in Scotland. They were awaiting trial in Scotland for numerous other charges and while we were in Armley Prison we spent our short time together talking about our defence for the conspiracy. I was still in patches at this time; while I was stationed at Armley I was still considered a high-risk prisoner. I was constantly being monitored and carefully watched by the prison guards. By this time, I had been a Christian eighteen months and during that period I'd had a life-changing experience with God.

My life had been completely changed for the better, it was while I was on the exercise yard one day that I had a strong conviction inside myself that I should change my plea from 'Not guilty' to 'Guilty'. I remembered what had happened at the trial for the robbery and shivered at the thought of having to make the same mistake twice. however, the thought persisted and I tried hopelessly to shrug them away from my mind. I started to feel really uncomfortable, especially when the idea continued to linger in my thoughts and wouldn't go away. I knew that I was guilty and that I'd committed the burglaries, but I was too afraid that my sentence would be increased even further if I pleaded guilty to the conspiracy charge.

When I returned to my cell that day the thought just wouldn't go away and I started to feel at unease with myself. My thoughts had turned towards God and I remembered everything that He had done for me since I'd become a Christian. I knew that I was a different person inside and my conscience was starting to get the better of me. I had an overwhelming feeling of guilt and I knew that I was being dishonest with myself, with the courts, and with God. I knew that the prosecution's evidence against me was all circumstantial and that there was a very strong possibility that I would be found 'Not guilty' if I decided to go through with the trial.

I struggled throughout the night with my conscience and I knew what I had to do, but it didn't stop me from trying to make a pact with God. It was a desperate prayer and I asked God whether he would be willing to turn a blind eye for that moment in court while I pleaded not guilty. That was the longest night of my life while I was waiting for Him to reply – but nothing happened. I was asking God to do the impossible and, even though God can do 'all things', including the impossible, I realised that this was one prayer He definitely wasn't going to answer the way I wanted Him to. I felt empty inside and I couldn't find any peace in my heart that night. I thought that I'd made God look cheap by attempting to bring Him down to my level and by trying to make Him turn a blind eye. I was still a new Christian and I had so much to learn about

God. The silence in my cell was deafening and in the end my conscience started to get the better of me.

I finally came to my senses and realised that I was being totally selfish. I asked God to forgive me for being so foolish. I prayed again, only this time I prayed in earnest and in humility. I asked God to give me the strength to make the right decision. I said that I would plead guilty when I went into the courtroom. It was at that exact moment when I started thinking about changing my plea that I felt a tremendous peace in my heart and mind. I knew that I had made the right decision, and even though it came at an enormous cost I felt as though I had God's approval and that He was smiling down towards me. For the rest of that night I managed to sleep like a little baby.

I woke up early the next day and was feeling totally refreshed and at peace with myself. I contacted my solicitor to arrange a meeting with my barrister before the trial started. When we met together in the Crown Courts a week later I was asked by my barrister whether I had changed my mind about pleading guilty and I said 'No', I hadn't changed my decision. If anything, I believed more strongly than ever that I was doing the right thing. Again, I was feeling that peace all around me and I felt God's presence in that cell.

While I was waiting down in the cell area for the trial to start, I thought I heard God saying clearly, 'I will not allow the sentence to be higher than three years.' I did a quick calculation in my head and thought to myself, 'Well, that's ten years in total.' I wondered whether I could cope with this, it was while I was thinking about this that I suddenly felt that there was an awesome presence of God around me in the cell. I could almost hear Him saying, 'Don't you worry about that because everything is going to be alright.' Wow! I felt as though a heavy weight had been lifted from my shoulders and although I was facing a huge mountain ahead I knew deep down inside that, with God's help, He was going to give me the strength to climb it.

When I arrived at the Crown Courts in Huddersfield I felt as though I was walking on cloud nine. As the trial started my barrister entered a 'Guilty' plea on my behalf and I was sent back to the prison to await sentencing. Rob and Harry both went through with the trial and at the end of the week they were both found guilty unanimously by a jury. We were gathered in the courts waiting to be sentenced, when the judge came back into the courtroom we knew by the look on his face that it didn't look good for us.

Judgement came quick and fast and before I realised it both my mates were being escorted downstairs after receiving heavy prison sentences. I was the last to be sentenced and stood facing the judge. I could feel the blood draining from my head when I thought to myself,' this geezer's going to hammer me with time,' and I waited to hear him pass sentence.

The judge was speaking for quite a while and I was thinking about God during that time. I was thanking Him for His promise and for Him being there in the dock with me. My attention was caught when I heard the judge mentioning about my role in the conspiracy. I heard him saying that, although I may not have been the instigator of the crimes, I was most definitely the perpetrator of them happening. And, although I was already serving a long prison sentence for the robbery, he couldn't help but feel that society needed to be protected from the likes of me. I felt history was repeating itself, though I wasn't too worried because deep down inside I knew in my heart that God had made a promise and that I had no doubt in my mind that He was going to keep it.

Finally, the judge finished with his summing up and continued with the sentencing. He started by saying, 'I would be sentencing you today for a total of seven years to run consecutively to the sentence that you are already serving, but because you pleaded guilty from the start of the trial I will reduce that sentencing to a maximum of five years. This means that your total sentence will be twelve years in prison.' I waited for him to continue, but he had finished his sentencing and the last thing that I heard from the courtroom was the judge's gavel hitting the desk and him ordering the prison guards to take the prisoner down to the cells.

I couldn't believe my ears and started to argue with the judge saying, 'But Your Honour, surely you haven't finished. Surely you've forgotten something else.' I had expected him to say, 'Oh yeah,' but he didn't and made it crystal clear that there had been no mistakes and that he hadn't forgotten anything.

I was flabbergasted and before I could say, 'I object, Your Honour,' I was quickly rushed down into the cell area. I couldn't understand what was happening and I felt absolutely gutted and let down by God. When the cell door closed shut and the prison guards went off for their break I just knelt down on my knees and asked, 'Why, God, have you tricked me into believing that honesty paid?' I couldn't control the way that I was feeling and I started to become angry. I thought to myself, 'Well, God, if you can't be trusted, then who can?' I even thought about giving up on my faith, but then I felt that strong feeling again where the presence of God was all around me. Suddenly I heard a gentle voice that was saying, 'I will never leave you, nor forsake you. I want you to put your trust in Me, and I will never let you down.'

I was completely overwhelmed by a feeling of complete love and found myself in a flood of tears. I said, 'Father God, I'm so sorry, I do believe in You, but You have got to help my unbelief. I do want to trust in You but I need to know, was it You that was saying "I will not let them sentence you to more than three years" or was it just my imagination? 'As I was saying this, I heard movement outside, and I realised that it was from the very minute that I had prayed this prayer. The cell door was quickly opened and my solicitor and barrister were standing there with their mouths wide open. My solicitor spoke and said, 'You must have somebody up there who loves you because the judge has asked for you to be brought back into the courtroom.'

Now I was intrigued and wanted to know what was going on. It was unheard of and I was wondering what I'd done wrong. I was lead back into the courtroom flanked by my prison guards and I was asked to stand in front of the judge. He looked at me for a while as though he'd just remembered something and then he started speaking. I couldn't remember most of what he was talking about but, then I heard him saying, 'I've reconsidered my decision and I feel that there may be a little unfairness in my sentencing. I recognise that you had changed your plea to "guilty" which came at a great cost to you, and it's because of this that I will recognise and respect your honesty. The sentence that I had originally sentenced you to for five years will not stand and I will therefore re-sentence you to a maximum of three years' imprisonment for your part in the conspiracy. This will bring the total sentence that you will serve to ten years' imprisonment.'

After hearing these words, I was jubilant and very close to doing a jig in the courtroom. I was smiling as though I'd just won the lottery which nobody could really understand. I must've thanked the judge about five times before I was taken downstairs to the cells. The last thing I can remember hearing was the judge commenting to one of the court officials, 'I've never known anybody be so happy at being sentenced to ten years in prison!' But little did he realise that I wasn't jubilant for that sole reason; I was walking on cloud nine because GOD HADN'T LET ME DOWN; HE HAD KEPT HIS PROMISE.

'Know therefore that the Lord your God is God; he is the faithful God, keeping his covenant of love to a thousand generations of those who love him and keep his commandments.' Deuteronomy 7:9

*   *   *   *

25

OUT OF PATCHES

The day after I was sentenced at Huddersfield Crown Court I was transferred straight back to Walton Prison. The governor at Armley Prison was relieved to be rid of me, but I didn't care because I knew that my life was about to take a whole new turning. I knew in my heart that God had proved beyond any doubt that He was there right by my side and my faith had been increased a hundred-fold when I witnessed what had happened in the courts. I felt that I could take on the whole world. Reality though soon hit home when I arrived back in Liverpool. I was brought before the governor at Walton who informed me that the very next day I would be coming off the Category E list and that I would be transferred to a top-security Category A prison at the first opportunity.

I thought that was fantastic news and I remember when I was returned to my old cell thinking how different things were going to be when I went back on to the main part of the prison. I'd spent twenty months locked up in a cell on my own without anybody else and I prayed that night, asking God whether it would be possible for me to be put in a cell with another Christian so that we could pray and read the Bible together. It was a simple prayer and I was relying on God to answer it. What I didn't realise was that God has a sense of humour.

When I'd asked God to put me in a cell with another Christian I didn't want to be padded up with somebody who was known or took drugs. Little did I realise it then but God had different plans. The following morning when I was taken out of patches I was put into a prison cell with one of the biggest and most well-known criminals in Liverpool. He had been sentenced to four and a half years inside prison for a three-quarters-of-a-million-pounds conspiracy and, not by chance, he was also one of the main heroin dealers in Liverpool. My heart started to sink with the thought of spending time with a known gangster and drug dealer but I guess that it was a big testing of my faith from the start.

Right from the beginning I decided that I would put my new cell mate in the picture and I told him that I was a born-again Christian. He said that he didn't mind as long as I didn't try and force my faith onto him. We spent six weeks together and during most of that time he didn't mind my talking about Jesus. I saw it as a great opportunity and during that short time I managed to share with him what had happened in my life. I not only witnessed to my pad-mate but I also managed to witness to the many inmates who regularly called around to the cell to buy heroin. I don't know what happened to him afterwards but what I do know is that he'd heard the truth about God and it was for him to decide whether or not it was real. It was his choice whether he wanted to believe it or not.

*　　*　　*　　*

PART SIX

26. WAKEFIELD PRISON

I was transferred to a maximum-security jail in Wakefield. I'd heard rumours about it being a real house of horrors I wasn't looking forward to going there at all. I didn't mind doing my sentence in a nice quiet prison, but to think that I was going to spend the next three years of my sentence living amongst murderers, rapists and child molesters, I couldn't bear thinking about it.

Stepping of the prison bus having just arrived at Wakefield, I knew that this place was going to be very different to all the other prisons that I'd been in. First impressions where it didn't seem too bad. I started making my way to the reception area I was trying to get a feel for the place, I just couldn't understand why everybody was being friendly. Even the screws were making the effort which I thought was really weird.

I knew that Wakefield housed some of the most dangerous men in the country and that the majority of inmates there were serving life, double life and natural life sentences. It felt as though I'd reached the end of the line. I walked into the reception area and was told to wait until an officer would come along to see me. I thought it was strange that I'd been left alone without having any guards around me and I started to feel a little paranoid. I was debating with myself whether or not I should start a fight in the reception so that I could be moved back to Liverpool, but I thought that I'd wait around and see what happened. After a while I started to think maybe it's not such a bad place after all.

While I was being processed at the reception I sat around minding my own business and reading my Bible. (And, praying under my breath!) I didn't want to enter into a conversation with anybody because I still felt suspicious of everybody and everything. Even though I was now a Christian, I still had areas in my life that God needed to deal with. I started to think to myself that I shouldn't be mixing with these kinds of people but, before I could think anymore, I heard my name being called and I went through the usual process of being booked into the prison.

After the interview, had finished the prison officer said that I'd be allocated a cell shortly. I was asked whether or not I wanted to take something out of a box which was at the end of the counter. I walked over to the box and I looked inside and was horrified when I saw a collection of craft knives. I immediately thought that they'd made a mistake and that I'd looked in the wrong place. But when the prison guard said that it was OK to take one I couldn't help but ask him, 'Why on earth should I need one of those?' I could feel the hairs standing up on the back of my neck when he grinned and replied, 'You'll need one of them for when you get in there.' He was pointing towards the main part of the prison. I didn't know whether to take him seriously or not. I just couldn't believe that they were handing out weapons and was wondering to myself just what kind of place had I come to?

I had a terrible gut feeling that I shouldn't be in that awful place and I soon found myself praying under my breath. I was asking God to help and arrange for me to be sent to another prison with a much more relaxed atmosphere. I didn't want to be there and attempted to point out to God that I was different and that the offences that I had committed were completely different in comparison to the other people here. It sounds ridiculous when you think about it, but it's true. I was trying to justify my sins by pointing towards somebody else's in the hope that it proved that mine weren't as bad and deserved a lighter approach.

I had so much to learn about God and it wasn't long before I realised how shallow and immature I was beginning to sound. It was really stupid to try and tell God what to do, once I realised this I suddenly felt a tremendous peace come flooding into my heart again. remembered God's promise in His word that He will never leave me, nor forsake me. I knew that God's presence was close by, so I stopped praying and opened my ears to listen to what He was saying.

> 'The LORD himself goes before you and will be with
> you; he will never leave you nor forsake you.
> Do not be afraid; do not be discouraged.'
> Deuteronomy 31:8

I didn't have to wait long and what I thought that God was saying was that His Holy Spirit was with me, and that I was in this place for a reason. Of course, God could have arranged for me to go to a more relaxed prison but there was still work for Him to do in my life and this was the place where all this work was going to happen. I didn't realise what He meant by this, but I trusted in Him and believed that no matter what happened while I was there He would not allow any harm to come to me. I prayed under my breath and said, 'Well, God, I don't know what's lying ahead, I believe strongly that You're with me and that You're in this place.'

I was allocated a cell on the infamous B Wing at Wakefield Prison. I knew lots of people within the prison but they were spread around on different wings. I knew that I'd meet up with them sooner or later and was unsure what was I going to say to them about my new-found faith. I wasn't afraid, but it felt a bit awkward because these men knew me from the outside. They knew what I was like because we had committed many crimes together, and the reputation that I had before I became a Christian had followed me everywhere regardless of whether I knew them or not.

I was soon called over to meet with one of the biggest gangsters in Manchester. He was serving ten years for armed robbery on several security vans in and around the Manchester area. Although I'd not worked for him in the past, he was aware of my reputation and had heard all about me. He wanted to meet to make sure that everything was all right and also to make me feel welcome. I didn't hesitate to tell him the truth about my faith in God. I shared my experiences with him and for an hour and half as he sat there and listened, I noticed that although he was quite interested and astounded by what he had heard, it just wasn't enough to convince him to go to church. We talked a little while longer and, after being offered some drugs and a little advice about the prison, I made my excuses and went on my way.

Obviously, I declined the offer of the drugs, but took on board the advice. It wasn't long before the word went around that I was one of the lads and, in a roundabout way, it warned other inmates not to mess around with me. I met up with lots of people that I knew from my past and many known criminals who I'd respected and looked up to when I was in my teenage years. I boldly witnessed to them also about Jesus and shared my story about how God had changed my life. Most of them were slightly interested, but were too set in their old way of life that the thought of any change for them was unthinkable. I continued witnessing to whoever I met and they started calling me 'John the Baptist'. I didn't care about this because as far as I was concerned I was doing what I believed God was calling me to do – and that was to go out into all the world and preach the gospel.

'Therefore, go and make disciples of all nations.'
Matthew 28:19

This was a great opportunity as I wasn't inside prison to make friends. My attitude was that I was just passing through this place without any plans to return. It wasn't long before I took advantage of the courses that were available in the prison. I enrolled in a course with the education department and I started to re-educate my mind by reading books, and was constantly studying and reading the Bible. Basically, I went back to school and studied English, Maths, Criminology, Psychology, and even Theology at an advanced level. I took on a catering course at a later stage when I was transferred to another prison, but this just added towards building myself up for when I was eventually released into the outside world.

The majority of inmates who serve big sentences take drugs in some form or another in order to help them get through their sentences. More often than not they would take drugs to escape from the reality of the situation that they're in, but what they don't realise is that sooner or later they have to come down from their highs and face up to their situation and deal with their problems.

I wasn't interested in taking drugs anymore and I knew that this was no longer a part of my life. God had done a great thing by taking the desire away from me so that I was totally free from this addiction. I still smoked tobacco, but this wasn't a major problem at the time. I started attending the prison Christian Fellowship meetings at Wakefield Prison and met with many other Christian inmates who'd had similar dramatic spiritual experiences and encounters with God. Their lives had been completely transformed by these experiences and it was a great opportunity to get together and to share what God was doing in our lives.

The power of God was moving throughout the prison system like a tidal wave and many people's lives were being transformed and changed in the twinkling of an eye. Hardened criminals were becoming 'born again' overnight and their lives were being completely and utterly transformed. There was such a mighty move of God's Holy Spirit that there were men queuing up to be baptised. The Bible teaches us that we must not only repent to God of our wrongful doings (sin) but that we must follow in the footsteps of Jesus and be baptised in water, in the same way that He was baptised.

'Then Jesus came from Galilee to the Jordan to be baptised by John.' Matthew 3:13

This caused quite a stir within the churches that were operating in the prison because they had different beliefs in this matter with regards to how a person should be baptised. The Catholics were arguing about this subject because they believed that you should be prayed over and sprinkled with water, whereas, on the other hand, the Church of England were equally convinced that you did it in a different way. The Methodists had their own views about baptism too and all this arguing and debating just complicated things even further and made it more difficult to get baptised at all.

In the meantime, the Pentecostals were getting on with the job at hand and were baptising the new converts in the prison bath which was in the shower room. The inmates were being baptised with full emersion in water. I was thinking that I should also be baptised at this time and talked with the minister about this. He told me that they could no longer baptise people in the shower room because there was a health and safety risk. To my surprise, he had spoken with the governor of the prison who would allow the local fire brigade to bring a big water tank into the exercise yard to baptise the inmates. I was really excited because I felt that it was my time to shine. Disappointingly this feeling was short lived because we heard that the church leaders from different faiths had started to complain to the governor about this and the controversy continued.

The governor finally caved in to pressure from the leaders of the other churches and decided to cancel the idea in order to keep the peace. Then suddenly, the baptisms were stopped completely by the governor because it was creating so many problems within the churches. The arguments continued and as a result nothing was achieved other than several inmates were missing out on the opportunity of being baptised. I felt disappointed but I thought, 'One day my time will come.' I'd been a Christian for two years and had never been given that opportunity until I arrived at Wakefield, and now that the opportunity had arrived I had missed out on it because of the division that was going on in the churches.

*   *   *   *

27

THE BLAZING SWORD

I became good friends with another Christian called Tom. He was a real character who arrived at Wakefield on a transfer from Frankland Prison. He was inside for armed robbery and was serving ten years like myself. He told me about how he had had an awesome experience whilst he was in the punishment block at Frankland. At first, he was a little reluctant to share his story because he thought that I may think he was barking mad. But, as we spent more time together, he finally relented and told me what had happened.

He shared about how when he was sentenced to ten years his partner had promised to stand by him faithfully. But, as time slowly passed by, he started to notice little cracks were forming in their relationship. It's a similar story that I'd heard hundreds of times with countless inmates and it wasn't too surprising when he revealed that his wife had been unfaithful to him. He went on to explain that his marriage was on the rocks and that he still had a few years left to serve on his sentence. It was more than he could bear and he tried desperately to keep things going in his relationship. This continued for another two years but, in the end, the marriage collapsed altogether and, like most cases, it ended up in the divorce courts.

Unfortunately, there were children involved and this made things much more difficult for Tom to come to terms with. He knew that his marriage was finished but he just couldn't handle losing his children too. It truly broke his heart and when he only had a year left to serve on his sentence he decided that he couldn't take any more. He told me how he was involved in a fight at Frankland Prison and that he had nearly killed another inmate. He said that it was as though all his frustrations were taken out on this man who wasn't even aware of what he was actually going through. The guards broke the fight up and Tom was dragged down into the punishment block. His fight didn't end there and whenever he could find an opportunity he would fight with the prison guards too.

It was a no win situation and he knew that his life was getting worse by the minute. He said that he had lost everything and that he felt that there was no reason for him to live anymore and even went as far as contemplating the idea of taking his own life. It was a sad story and I really felt for him at the time, but what I heard next just knocked me off my feet. I was astounded by what I heard. He continued by telling me that, on that same day, he had firmly decided that he would take his own life. He waited until night time came and, when the cell lights were turned out for the evening, he pulled out the blade that he had kept hidden. Without giving it any more thought he slashed both of his wrists.

There was blood oozing out thick and fast, and he said that it was in that very moment when he was about to lose consciousness that he knew that he was going to die. And suddenly there was a great flash of white light that dazzled him to near blindness. He covered his eyes but then he became aware of somebody else being present in the cell. When he looked in front of him he saw an enormous angel who was dressed in full battle gear and whose hands were holding onto a huge sword that was blazing like a fire. He said that at this time he became very afraid and fell to his knees and was trying to look away in fear of his life.

The angel suddenly withdrew his sword in one swift movement and a blazing light started to move quickly in Tom's direction. It swished past his head and just as quickly as the sword was drawn out of its scabbard it was returned in a flash of a second. The angel looked at him for a short while and then, before Tom could blink his eyes, the angel had disappeared from sight leaving him in total darkness. When suddenly, the room was filled with another bright light and this time he heard God's voice who was speaking to him. God told him that He loved him and that He didn't want him to feel that there was no hope for his life. There and then God filled Tom's heart with His love and the reassurance that everything was going to be all right.

He became aware that everything was back to normal in the cell and that his wounds had stopped bleeding. Although there was still a huge of amount of blood spread around the floor and over the walls of the cell, he didn't feel as though he was in any immediate danger. He said that he went to sleep that night with a peace in his heart that he'd never had before. He told me that even though he wasn't sure about what the future held for him, that he firmly believed that indeed 'everything was most certainly going to be alright'. From that moment on he just knew in his heart that his life was never going to be the same.

The experience had completely changed his life around and he immediately requested a transfer to another prison to start afresh and to help him rebuild his life. He was on fire for Jesus when he arrived at Wakefield and he constantly witnessed to other inmates about his faith. We spent many months working together as a team inside the prison and continued to pray for God to move and bring His revival to the many men who didn't know Him. Although Tom came from Manchester he had Irish descendants who came from staunch Catholic backgrounds. We wouldn't always meet eye to eye on matters relating to the Church and would sometimes disagree with each other on certain issues, but we were both young Christians and had a lot to learn. Our friendship was very strong because we bonded together like brothers and we would soon put our differences to one side.

Eventually he was released from prison and although it was sad to see him leave, it was also a happy moment and a time of celebration for us both because he was the first that was getting out of prison starting on a whole new journey in life. We both knew that this time there was a huge difference and advantage that was going in his favour because this time he wasn't alone: he had Jesus in his heart and a great God to lead him wherever He called him to be. It was a privilege to have met with this amazing brother in Christ and when I think about his story I can't help but feel what an awesome and amazing God we serve.

28

GETTING CLOSER TO GOD

I was reading my Bible one day when I started to think about my relationship with God. Over the years while I'd been inside prison I'd accumulated a large collection of books, audio tapes, and personal items such as letters, family photos, etc. I wanted to get closer to Him. While I was thinking about this I came to the conclusion that comforts I had around me were a distraction, and if I didn't have these possessions it would be a real opportunity for me to experience God in a more personal way. I decided to give this a go, and made plans to clear my prison cell of everything that I felt was a distraction.

Inside prison every item that you have in your possession has been a privilege which has been given to you by the prison. Sometimes you have to fight tooth and nail to get some of the luxury items, such as decent furniture, curtains, bedding, clothes, etc. You could sometimes wait months for an inmate to vacate his cell where there may be a decent bedside cabinet or writing table to become available. I'd collected a reasonably decent array of furniture and my cell was looking quite smart during the time that I was at Wakefield, but to everybody's surprise, I started giving all these items away to other inmates. What had taken me months to collect together, took only minutes to clear away.

My prison cell was looking quite bare within a very short period of time, I wasn't finished there. I decided to finish the job and went down to the PO's office with several boxes that were full to the brim with my personal items. There are usually at least two screws inside the wing office always so when I walked into the office they were more surprised that I requested I put all my stuff back into my private property. Usually it's the other way around where inmates are requesting items to be released from their private property. It had never happened before and they didn't know how to handle it. At first, they tried to talk me out of it, but in the end, they accepted my unusual request.

There was absolutely nothing left in my cell except the bed, the clothes that I was wearing, and my Bible. I went back down to the office and asked for the bed to be removed from the cell. I was finally allowed this but was told that I had to keep the mattress in there at least for a while. Everybody thought that I'd lost the plot and was taking things too far, but I was determined to get closer to God and felt this was the right way at that time. That night when they locked the door I shoved the mattress into the corner of the cell and started to read my Bible. I read it for several days and prayed and fasted for God to reveal Himself to me. Whenever the cell door was opened I just closed it straight away because I didn't want to be disturbed.

I was reading in the Old Testament a story about how Elijah was eating the word of God and how it tasted like sweet honey. I started to read large passages from the New Testament in the Bible, and after reading it repeatedly, I started to eat the word of God. I know this sounds crazy, but it was true. I was literally eating large chunks of the Bible and it started to taste like honey. I was meditating and reading the word one day when I came across the scripture describing the presence of God as being like that of a sweet-smelling aroma. I closed my eyes and as I sat there a powerful aroma filled the entire cell. I could feel electricity in the air and, at the same time I could hear it crackling, I knew that God was there inside the cell. Even though I was at total peace with myself, I was too afraid to open my eyes.

'Come, all you who are thirsty, come to the waters;
and you who have no money, come, buy and eat.'
Isaiah 55:1

It was a fantastic experience and was something that I felt that I wanted to do for myself. I wouldn't suggest to anyone else to follow in my footsteps because it was a personal thing that I wanted to pursue. Through this I learnt that if you really want to get closer to God that if you seek Him with all your heart He will meet with you half way. I agree that eating large portions of the Bible was a ridiculous idea, but I wanted to be so close to God – and if that's what it took to get His attention then I didn't mind doing it.

Of course, there are other ways to seek after God and I'm sure He will meet with you wherever you are. I've experienced God in many other different ways and I've found that if it's your heart's desire to meet with Him then God will spend time with you. After a period of time, I started to ask for my personal possessions to be returned to my cell, but I kept it to a minimum because I wanted to keep focused on God and for Him to remain closer to me.

*   *   *   *

29

GERRY THE ARTIST

Gerry was serving eighteen years for kidnapping and torturing his victim. He had served twelve years of his sentence and was refused parole from the Home Office. He had spent most of his childhood being moved around from one foster home to another. When I first met with him he said that when he was younger he was always getting into trouble with the police and although he was arrested several times he was never charged with anything because of his young age. He said that he would just be returned to whichever foster home he was living in until eventually, one day, he had finally reached the age where he was old enough to be charged. He was arrested for several violent assaults and after numerous court appearances he was finally sent to an adult prison.

He had a string of convictions which were mainly through violence that followed him all through his life. He was a repeat offender and he told me that his life was like a vicious circle that he couldn't seem to break free from. As a result, he spent most of his young adult life inside prison. He went on to explain that he'd spent so much time inside prisons that he felt that he had started to become institutionalised. He mentioned that he was an atheist and that he didn't believe that God existed. However, whenever I spent time with him he always listened and had lots of questions about my faith. I found it really challenging but, it was hard work when you're trying to explain about God to somebody who didn't even believe that He really existed.

Over a period of time I came to realise that he wasn't interested in hearing about God and was being as stubborn as a mule. He had made it quite clear that his beliefs wouldn't change unless God himself jumped out in front of him. I thought about this and decided that I'd give him time to think more about what we had discussed. It sounds strange to say but even inside prison I found that my time was a precious commodity and that the time that I'd spent with him talking about God could've been put to better use. I thought to myself that there's always somebody who's willing to listen. So, I left him to his own devices and decided to call it a day. He was an artist and would make a small living on the paintings and pictures that he did for the inmates. He also sold drugs and tobacco from his prison cell which helped him live quite comfortably within the prison.

I read a book one day about an American girl who was born into a rich family in the United States. She was very independent from her family and from an early age she started to build up businesses of her own; she was very successful in everything that she tried. The story went on to describe how her business associates were so jealous of her successes that they conspired together to steal her wealth and fortune. She was finally kidnapped and tortured until she signed over all her assets and money. Eventually, when they had completely drained her of millions of dollars, they plotted together to commit the final act in their plan: to murder this young woman and to leave no witnesses.

It was a brilliant book to read and it had a fantastic ending where God moved miraculously in her life and saved her from certain death. The would-be assassins were all caught and were soon brought to justice. After I read this amazing story my immediate thoughts were towards Gerry who I thought would find it an interesting read himself. So, just before everybody was banged up for the night I called around to his cell. He wasn't there so I decided to leave the book lying on the top of his bed. In the meantime, he was downstairs with the prison probation officer. It was his last opportunity for parole and it was the final interview before the reports were forwarded to the Home Office.

The interview wasn't going in his favour and when reports from the prison psychiatrists and psychologists were discussed, the probation officer tried to explain that they had covered every aspect of his life from childhood to the present day and that there was no hope for him for the future. His violent behaviour and track record had followed him throughout his sentence and nothing had really changed to convince the parole board to release him into the outside world. It just happened that the probation officer was a Christian and before Gerry could react to this latest piece of news he said that he was sorry and that he would pray for him as a last resort.

It was like a volcano had erupted when we heard the shouting and swearing coming from the other side of the prison. Apparently, he hadn't taken the news lightly, but the last comment from the probation officer had made him see red. He stormed out of the office and was threatening to return in five minutes; he swore that he was going to kill the probation officer with an iron bar. We could see that there was a sudden rush of activity with the screws moving around the wing hastily locking everybody into their cells while they tried to calm the situation down.

I heard him storming his way upstairs and thought to myself that he needs to calm down otherwise he's going to get himself nicked. While he was searching around in his cell for a weapon I heard his door was slammed shut. At that point everybody had expected him to kick off and start smashing up his pad but instead everything went quiet. It was weird because there wasn't a sound coming from his direction and, after nearly three hours had passed by, still nothing had happened.

I was sat reading a book and at around midnight I heard an almighty scream; I knew that it was definitely coming from his direction. So, I rushed to the window and was trying to make sense of what was happening but then I realised that the shouting had turned into laughing and it seemed as though he was crying at the same time. At first nobody knew what he was saying, but it became clearer and all you could hear that was coming from his cell were the words, 'He's real! Oh, Lord Jesus is real!'

I looked through my window and I could see that there was a sea of faces pressed up close to their windows. All of them were listening intently, wondering what was happening. In between the laughing and the crying, we heard that he was singing at the top of his voice, and was saying, 'PRAISE THE LORD,' and 'THANK YOU, JESUS!' It was obvious to me now that he was having a tremendous spiritual experience with God and I couldn't help but smile to myself and wonder how on earth this had come about. The singing went on right throughout the night and it wasn't until early the next morning that I found out exactly what had happened.

I was just waking up when the prison started to come to life. I heard the jangling of keys and I could hear the cell doors being opened. I had hardly got out of bed when my door was suddenly pushed open and Gerry came running in with a toothy grin that would've made Bugs Bunny feel proud. He threw his arms around me and was still singing, and laughing, and jumping around like a little child.

It turned out that when somebody had slammed the cell door shut the night before, Gerry was in a murderous rage. He was desperately searching around his cell for the nearest weapon when the door was closed. He was about to release all his anger by breaking the place apart when his eyes were diverted and had rested on the book that was placed on the top of his bed. He said, 'It was as though something had arrested me in my spirit,' and then, suddenly, he became very calm. He edged his way towards the bed and picked up the book whilst wondering to himself how on earth it had gotten there. Something much more spectacular happened when he realised that he had the pressing need to sit down and read it.

When he had finished reading this remarkable story he said that 'the tears were running down my face and that I felt terribly guilty and remorseful for the many crimes that I had committed in my life', especially the grotesque kidnapping and torturing of the victim of his latest offence. He commented on some of the things that it spoke about in the book and said that when he realised that God had saved the young woman from being murdered by her kidnappers it was just too much for him to handle and that was the reason that he felt such a strong conviction in his heart.

He also shared that it was at that very moment when he was overwhelmed with shame and guilt that he realised that there was somebody else who was stood there right by his side. He said, 'When I looked to my left side I could see a man in white robes who was just stood there and was smiling in my direction. When I looked at him I was afraid at first, but when the man asked me if I knew who he was, I knew in my heart straight away that the man that I was looking at in my prison cell was Jesus, even though I had never met Him in person before.'

In the Bible, we read the story in Acts 9:1–19 about a man called Saul who persecuted the early Christian Church. He was a man with great authority and had very strong convictions in his faith that the new believers in Christ were blaspheming against God and were teaching heresies – ideas that went against the accepted religious beliefs of the time – to the people. He set off on a journey to kill as many of the so-called heretics of the new faith, but while he was travelling on the road he was suddenly confronted by a brilliant, blinding bright light. He became very afraid and was terrified when he heard a voice that came from heaven. It said, 'Saul, Saul, why do you persecute Me and kill My people', he realised that it was the voice of God and became even more frightened than ever.

God had arrested him in his spirit that day, and had stopped him from committing a terrible crime. When I heard Gerry's story I realised that it was a similar story to what had happened to Saul on the road to Damascus. God had prevented him from carrying out his murderous intentions to harm the probation officer who was a Christian and who belonged to God. I believe that God protects those who are His, it wasn't a coincidence when the door was slammed shut that night because God wanted to meet with Gerry, even though Gerry never expected such a thing would happen in his life time.

It was an incredible story to believe even for me as a Christian, but I knew that what he was sharing was a true account of what had happened in his cell that night. He finished by saying, 'When I realised that God truly loved me and wanted to forgive me for all that I'd done in my life, I couldn't help but fall onto my knees before him and surrender my life to Jesus.' It says in the Bible that if you call on the name of Jesus and truly repent from all your wrong doings then you will be saved and you will be forgiven. I believe that Gerry the artist had made a genuine commitment to God that night and had given his heart to Jesus.

'For "Everyone who calls on the name of the Lord will be saved."' Romans 10:13

While he shared this remarkable story, I was looking intently at his face and I noticed that his whole appearance had changed and that his face was radiant. I saw with my own eyes a hardened criminal who had been totally broken by the obvious and clear love of God without any human interference. I also witnessed that he had received a true revelation of Jesus and of God's love that night, and although his face was wet with tears, they were not tears of sorrow, of anguish and pain, but they were genuine and unadulterated tears of joy. A complete freedom that he had received from Christ Jesus.

*   *   *   *

30

MAD MAX

In the late part of the eighties there was a burglary committed on a manor house in London that went tragically wrong. Three thieves broke into the property with the intention of stealing money and jewellery. It turned out that the owners were at home at the time of the burglary and they interrupted the burglars. They were tied up during the operation and, without going into too much detail, it ended up that the owners were murdered in their own home. One of the burglars, Max, was eventually sentenced to three life sentences for his part in the murders. His co-accused were also charged with murder and were both sentenced to life in prison.

When he first arrived at Wakefield, Max was allocated a cell on B Wing which was just a few doors away from mine. When I walked out of my cell that morning I noticed that it was unusually quiet for that time of day. There would normally be lots of inmates who would be rushing around on their way to their workplace or busying themselves with the hustle and bustle of prison life. However, this day was different and I soon found out why. I noticed that the new inmate had arrived at the prison. I first saw him when he was walking towards the wing office with his kit under his arms. While I was watching, him I noticed that most of the inmates were trying to avoid talking with him and were walking off in different directions. I could see that there was genuine fear on their faces as they walked away and I caught myself thinking, 'But he's only human.'

You could cut the atmosphere with a knife. I started to feel sorry for him while others were watching him from a distance and were obviously talking about the new arrival. He was the main subject of conversation on the wings and there were many stories being circulated about him before he arrived at Wakefield. They were obviously based on rumours that simply weren't true. The biggest story circulating the wing was that while he was on remand waiting for his trial to begin he had borrowed a book from another inmate. After a few days, the inmate who had lent him the book innocently paid him a visit and had asked whether he had finished reading it. When he was invited into Max's cell the inmate didn't realise that he was in any danger and, without thinking, he walked straight into a trap. The story went that when the inmate walked into the cell he was stabbed to death and stuffed under the bed.

A while later another inmate realised that his mate was still inside the cell. He knocked on the door and asked for his friend. Max just smiled and said that yes, he was inside and invited the second unsuspecting inmate into his cell. It wasn't until about half an hour later that Max supposedly calmly walked along to the wing office and informed the landing officers by saying, 'I think you'd better check my cell, boss, because you'll find there are two inmates there who won't be counted at roll call.' Now whether there was any truth in that story I couldn't really say, but it was something that had followed him around wherever he went and whatever prison he ended up being sent to.

In the meantime, I continued with life as normal and carried on going to the church. I was attending the prison Christian Fellowship meetings and was constantly witnessing to many inmates about Jesus. There wasn't anybody that I thought was unreachable for Christ and I didn't hesitate in speaking with anybody who was willing to listen. Until one day when I had a feeling that God was stopping me in my tracks and challenging me in that area. I felt that God was speaking to me about Max and was reminding me that although he had committed those horrible crimes, God still loved him and was willing to forgive him for everything as long as he was truly sorry.

Now I'd heard about the rumours and I didn't know what to believe when I was told the gory details. I wasn't afraid of anybody, at least that's what I thought until I thought about Max. The very idea of turning up at his cell door sent shivers down my spine. I immediately thought that it was a stupid idea and I tried to ignore what I thought God was saying. Surely, I reasoned to myself, God could find somebody else who could do this job better than I could? But the thought wouldn't go away and was constantly playing on my mind. I struggled with this for at least a week and I kept on putting it off by using all kinds of excuses like not finding the right opportunity or the exact moment where we could meet and talk.

In reality I was caught up in the fear of what would happen if he didn't like what I had to say. Then there was another type of fear and that was what would happen if I missed this opportunity altogether and I didn't tell him what he should hear. I was a Christian and it was my duty to share my faith – without fear – with whomever God brought me into contact with. I knew that God had not failed me this far and I realised, too, that no matter how difficult a situation was, God would never allow anything bad to happen to me. I knew what I had to do, and after saying a quick prayer I didn't hesitate any longer because I had found the strength inside and made my way to his cell.

I stood outside his door for a while and knocked quietly hoping that he wasn't in (I was still nervous), when suddenly, the cell door was opened. It was Max and when he invited me into his cell I could feel my knees were knocking together – I just hoped that he couldn't hear them! I was even more nervous when he closed the cell door almost shut and asked me to sit on the edge of the bed. The first thing I noticed when I walked into the cell was how meticulously clean everything was. The walls were spotless and didn't have the usual smut and pornography staring you in the face. I noticed that there were a couple of family photos on the picture board and that there were also smaller photos and little cards spread around on the bedside cabinets.

The bed was made in military style and the floor was so clean that I felt you could almost eat your dinner off it. I'd almost forgotten why I was there until he interrupted the silence by saying, 'How can I help you?' I remembered the previous night when I was praying about what to say and I felt that God wanted me to tell him that He loved him and not only did God forgive him for what he had done but that God also wanted to set him free. I could feel my heart was beating louder than the silence. It was an eerie silence and part of me wanted to leave, but Max was less than two feet away and he was waiting for a reply. I was thinking to myself that if I didn't answer any second I was going to be killed.

I finally remembered the reason why I was there and, taking one final gulp of faith, I started to share what God had put on my heart. When I had finished speaking there was a deadly silence in the room. My last comment was still ringing in my ears and that was when I mentioned about how God wanted to set this man free. Here I was sat in front of a convicted killer who was never going to be released from prison, and I was telling him that Jesus wanted to set him free. I wanted to leave now, but I'd come this far and I wanted to see what his response was going to be, so I decided to hang on in there.

He just looked at me. But while I was thinking about bolting for the door, he broke the silence and said, 'John, look I understand that you're a Christian and what you're attempting to do. I've been watching you for some time and think that you are genuine in what you say. I appreciate something dramatic has happened in your life, and that's great to hear, but I don't want to talk about this any further and I will think about what you've said.'

I thought to myself, 'Great, I've passed on the message, God, maybe it's a good idea that I leave now, 'as I was just about to make an exit when he laid a gentle hand on me and said matter-of-factly, 'It's because I respect you that I've listened to what you've said but if that had been anybody else I would've killed him.' I could tell he was serious when he said it and I didn't doubt that for one minute. I said, 'Cheers mate,' and with a big sigh of relief I quickly left and went straight back to my cell.

A few weeks went by and nothing seemed to have happened with Max and I couldn't understand why. I didn't know what to expect really, but I thought that it would at least have triggered something in his mind – enough to bring him to church. Nothing happened, as the weeks continued to pass by, I started to question myself: Did I really go into his cell and pass on that message, or was it all in my imagination? Surely, I didn't imagine it. I was thinking of giving it another shot, but I decided that I didn't want to push things with him. So, I just prayed about his situation and left it with God.

I heard through the grapevine a few weeks after leaving Wakefield Prison that Max had started going to the prison chapel and that he had finally given his life to Jesus.

* * * *

PART SEVEN

31. FEATHERSTONE PRISON

After serving twenty months at Wakefield Prison I was called into the PO's office and informed that I was going to be transferred to a Category C prison. This was great news as it meant that I was a step closer to being released from prison. I'd applied earlier in the year for parole, which was my second attempt, but I was turned down by the Home Office – it came as no big surprise. But, now that I was going to a Cat C nick I was more hopeful for a successful outcome on my next application.

I was really looking forward to the change of surroundings. I'd spent nearly two years in a place that was heavily fortified with razor wire and security cameras. It was a prison that was run on paranoia and it was almost suffocating at times. I'd never felt so claustrophobic about anything until I arrived at Wakefield Prison.

The transfer day finally arrived and I was all packed and ready to leave. It was a beautiful summer's day when I was put into a taxi along with two prison officers. We were driven through the countryside which felt quite strange after spending so much time in a maximum-security prison. Featherstone prison is located in the Midlands near Wolverhampton. I'd never heard of this place until I was told that I was being transferred there.

I thought the inmates were messing around when they said that the prison was right in the middle of the Black Country. (I wasn't even aware there was a place called the Black Country.) But when we arrived I soon found out that they were telling the truth.

I couldn't believe it, after I was booked into the prison, I was escorted by just one guard who pointed me in a certain direction and told me to make my own way to the office. He walked away and I was just left standing there with my kit under my arms, wondering to myself, 'What should I do now?' I thought it was strange, but it was a Category C prison, after all, and followed his instructions. I waited for another guard to let me through the gates and I made my way down a very long corridor, which was called the M6.

I remember walking along marvelling at my new-found freedom when I was approached by three other inmates. They asked which prison I'd come from and whether I had any drugs. I said that I didn't have any and before I could say, 'I'm a Christian,' they were offering to sell me some drugs, but I wasn't interested. I told them that I was drug free and started to walk away towards the office at the top of the landing.

I was approached by several other inmates who were trying to sell me their drugs – and all this happened before I'd managed to find the office. I thought to myself that I'd never seen so much activity in such a short space of time.

I was allocated a cell on one of the houses and once I'd unpacked all my stuff I thought I'd venture out of my cell and have a closer look at my new surroundings. Featherstone was separated into five blocks that were called houses, each house held around two hundred inmates. I was placed in House Four which was close to the M6.

My first port of call was to find out where the chapel was located and it didn't take me long to find it. I met with the prison chaplain there and introduced myself but he seemed rather busy and not really interested, so I left and wandered off down the landings. I noticed that the majority of inmates were of black or Asian origins. Although there were some white inmates, they were the minority and were few and far between. I tried to get a feel for the place and struck up conversations with lots of inmates. I asked about the prison and they filled me in with the general info, which I half knew anyway. I then asked about the spiritual welfare of the prison and they just looked at me and thought that I'd just arrived from another planet!

However, they did say that the chaplaincy team weren't interested in the prisoners' welfare and tended to hide themselves behind the four walls of the chapel. I heard that they were terrified of coming onto the main part of the prison and would only visit an inmate's cell if there were a death in the family or they were the bearers of some other bad news. Even then they were usually escorted around by a prison officer for their own safety. I found this really disturbing and unfortunately, I would soon find out for myself that what they were saying was true. When I arrived at Featherstone I didn't know any

157

other Christians who I could confide in. That night, when the cell doors were closed, I knelt on my knees and prayed for God to move in the prison.

I asked Him to bring the genuine born-again Christians together so that we could pray. I remember reading my Bible and read a scripture from the Old Testament where God said He would send someone 'from the north' (Isaiah 41:25). I was thinking about this reading when I finally fell asleep. The next morning when I woke up I heard a knock on my cell door. When I opened the door, I found that there were two inmates standing there with big smiles on their faces. They introduced themselves as Christians and said that they had both just arrived from separate prisons from the north of England; when they arrived the night before they had prayed for God to bring them into contact with the Christians inside the prison. I couldn't believe it and I knew that God had answered my prayers. I invited them into my cell and they shared their stories about how they had become Christians and I was amazed.

*　　*　　*　　*

32

BILLY WHIZZ

Billy was an ex whizz 'ed who had been addicted to speed (amphetamines) for many years and had ended up being arrested and charged with rape. He'd always denied the offence and claimed that he was innocent but the courts didn't agree and sentenced him to seven years in prison. He had already served two years of his sentence and he was finding things really difficult to cope with. One day he decided that he'd had enough and felt that he couldn't go on anymore. He made a decision that he was going to kill himself and when the doors were closed that night he waited for the lights to be turned off. While he was sitting at the end of his bed the cell was suddenly filled with a brilliant white light. He then noticed that somebody was standing next to him and he saw that it was a man who was holding His hands out in front of Him and was saying, 'Look, Billy, I did this for you.' When he managed to look closer he could see that there were scars visible in the palms of His hands. It was then that he realised that this man was Jesus.

He threw himself down onto the floor he wept bitterly at first, but then he cried like a little child. He knew that his life was an absolute mess and he had never considered God throughout his early years. He knew that God Himself was in that prison cell and had shown him mercy. Jesus had shown him the scars on

His hands and it had such an impact on Billy that he didn't hesitate to ask for His forgiveness – the rest is history. It changed his life forever, wherever he went he shared his faith with anybody who was willing to listen. It wasn't long after that experience in his cell that he was transferred to Featherstone Prison.

We started to meet together in my cell and prayed that God would bring other Christians together so that we could pray for revival in the prison. It wasn't long before other Christians were arriving at Featherstone from all different parts of the country. It was like an Exodus was taking place and God was preparing to do a great thing in the prison. After around three weeks there were about fifteen inmates meeting in my cell and all of them had amazing stories to tell. We prayed for the prisoners and their families, it wasn't long before we started to get positive results and answers to prayers.

The cells in Featherstone weren't big enough to hold any more people and we had an idea to approach the governor of the prison to ask permission to use the recreation room for our meetings. At first, he was reluctant, because the room wasn't being used, we were finally allowed to meet up at association time which was during the evening. It was a fantastic opportunity to share our faith and to fellowship together without any interruptions. The other inmates weren't particularly bothered about a few Christians meeting together but slowly yet surely some started to join our meetings and, after hearing the men's stories, they too made a decision and gave their hearts to Jesus.

The fellowship was rapidly growing and after a month there were around fifty inmates who were joining together, singing Christian songs, and sharing their own stories about how God had been answering their prayers. It was amazing to be a part of what was happening and to witness how God was bringing revival to the prison. It was as though a fire had started and it all began with prayer. The prison had its own chapel, but nobody went into those meetings because they felt that God wasn't in there. He was right there on the wings with the inmates and was doing great things in so many people's lives.

*   *   *   *

33

TIM'S STORY

There was an inmate called Tim who was selling cannabis for a drugs dealer in the prison. He started to attend the meetings on a regular basis. Although he wasn't a Christian, he felt that something spectacular was happening with lots of the inmates who he'd known for months. Never one to miss out on an opportunity, he made sure that if something was meant to happen for him then he didn't want that opportunity to pass him by. He was just a regular type of guy and was selling drugs just to help make life more comfortable for himself in the prison. His problem was that he liked his drugs too much and it wasn't long before he fell behind on his repayments and started to smoke all the profits.

He had attended a meeting that day and had heard that *'if you called on the name of Jesus'* then He would answer you. He stayed till the end of the meeting and then made his way back to his cell. He later shared this story when he became a Christian himself and it was truly remarkable to hear. When he arrived back at his cell he knew that he was in trouble because word had got around that he was going to get a visit from the drugs supplier to whom he owed a considerable amount of money. He wasn't a fighter and he knew that he was going to receive a terrible beating later that evening because he had smoked away all the last batch of cannabis which he was meant to sell.

Around 9.00pm that evening three heavies turned up at his cell – and they weren't there to have a social chat. He told us the next day at the meeting that when the dealer came into the cell he knew that he was in for a good kicking and, at worst, he could end up being knifed in the process or come away with a few broken bones. The two henchmen were standing guard at the cell door while the other came inside and demanded the money for the drugs. Tim couldn't offer an explanation and resigned himself to the fact that this whole thing was about to get real nasty, especially when the dealer pulled out a blade and started walking in his direction.

As the inmate lifted his hand backwards to strike the fatal blow, Tim recalled the conversation that went on earlier in the meeting and, knowing that he had nothing to lose whatsoever, he shouted out the name of Jesus. It stunned his assailant and, for a split second, he withdrew his hand. Surprisingly he put away the knife as though he'd had second thoughts. Astounded by this complete change in attitude Tim had asked what was going to happen next. Without any real explanation or further words being exchanged between them, the inmate picked up an old radio from the side of his bed which was broken and said out loud, 'This will do,' and he walked out of the cell holding it in his hand.

Tim was gob-smacked by this, and realised that it was true and it had worked for him. He had *called on the name of Jesus* and Jesus had answered him immediately. He shared this little story with us at the next meeting and finished off by telling us that, without thinking any further, he had thrown himself to his knees and had given his heart to Jesus right there and then where the inmate had stood and was about to scar him forever.

There were many more exciting stories to hear about, enough to fill another book. We had an amazing time to witness to many inmates who had broken lives which were being mended and had started to come together again.

* * * *

34

BARNEY THE BEAR

I was working in the kitchens at Featherstone Prison and was allocated the job of washing the pots. It was tedious work but I had to start somewhere and it paid good money. It was while I was working in the kitchens that I first encountered a lad called Barney. He was a short, stocky guy and was built like ten brick houses. He had a reputation in the prison for fighting, and although he was quite threatening to some inmates, I noticed that deep down inside there was a gentler side to his nature. I could see that Barney was a real character and typical of most inmates who spent as much time as they could working-out in the prison gym.

I'd never really had any dialogue with Barney but the opportunity arose while I was busy washing the prison pots one morning. As usual we had started the day with a quick coffee and while we were in the changing rooms he was talking to some of the younger inmates. I heard him bragging about his exploits about some of the fights that he'd been involved with. He seemed to have a captive audience and the more they listened the bigger his ego became. He had muscles like Popeye The Sailor Man and often flexed them to impress others. I remember thinking to myself that I wouldn't want to be on the receiving end of one of his punches. It would most probably knock me into kingdom come, and anybody else for that matter.

We started work after the coffee break, while the kitchen staff and inmates prepared the food for later that day, I was busy washing away at the pots. I was feeling good that morning so while I was working I started singing Christian songs to myself quietly in the corner. After a short while I was in full flow with my work and so was my singing as it became a little louder. I was scrubbing away with the washing so much so that I wasn't aware of the commotion taking place several feet behind me. It turns out from what others told me later, that while I was busy singing away like I didn't have a care in the world, Barney was standing directly behind me and was screaming and shouting at the top of his voice frantically demanding that I stopped.

He was working with the large vats in the kitchen and had piles of uncooked beetroot ready to throw into the boiling water. He was obviously unhappy that I was chirping away and enjoying my work, but something had snapped inside him which eventually brought the whole kitchen to a complete standstill. Barney only had one eye I don't think that though that would have mattered much because he was stood only 6 feet away from where I was working. So, while he was hollering for me to 'shut up' I was oblivious, and carried on with my work. He was getting really agitated, he picked up several large beetroots to throw in my direction. The first missile that he threw was a dead cert to hit its target. It was aimed at the back of my head but, as it reached within a foot of me, it had somehow miraculously steered off in a different direction. The same happened with the second, the third, and the fourth beetroot. None of them, although thrown with such ferocity and precision, had hit the target for which it was intended.

After a few more minutes I stopped working to clear the sweat from my eyes, it was then when I looked up that I noticed that there were red patches splotched all around me and up against the walls. I wondered innocently to myself how on earth that had happened as the walls weren't looking like that when I started. I turned around and noticed Barney was standing there right behind me with a handful of beetroots. I also noticed that his face had turned as red as the beetroots! Before I could ask what was happening he had stormed off in the direction of the restroom without another word being said. I looked at the other inmates who were just stood there saying nothing with their mouths wide open.

It was deadly silent in the kitchen and I soon realised that everybody was looking at me as though they'd seen a ghost. I decided to find out what all the fuss was about. After drying myself off, I went into the restroom to confront Barney about what had happened. I had a sneaky suspicion that he was the culprit and that I was going to find out the reason real soon. When I went into the back room I was expecting some kind of confrontation but what I found was the complete opposite. I found him crouched down near the floor quietly sobbing for some reason. I didn't understand why so I just asked him if everything was all right, when he finally looked in my direction he couldn't hold back the tears any more.

I thought to myself, 'Well, something strange has happened here!' So, I just waited for a few minutes for him to calm down. When he could compose, himself he managed to tell me his side of the story. He started by saying how he had been watching me for several weeks and couldn't figure out why I was so happy. He knew that I was a Christian, but he had heard all that stuff before inside prison and had seen many inmates making a mockery out of the Church, even though they themselves professed to be Christians. He told me that there was something different about me, but he just couldn't put his finger on it. I didn't say anything and just let him continue telling his story.

He said that most of the inmates he'd met and had attended the church in prison were hypocrites because their lifestyles away from church didn't seem to fit in with their beliefs. Understandably, he saw Christianity as a way of escape for most inmates and that it was another way and means for them to be released early on parole. What a damning indictment, I thought to myself, but unfortunately, he was speaking the truth. There are prisoners who attend church inside prison in the hope that it would help them to be released early. That's not the case because a prisoner's length of sentence is determined by the seriousness of his crime; no amount of church attendance is going to get them released any earlier than their EDR (earliest date of release) which is stated on their prison release papers.

He continued and told me that it was because of this that he believed that all Christians must be the same. He also said that after watching my movements in the prison for several weeks, he finally realised that there was something different about me. And although he had his doubts at first about Christianity, he came to the conclusion that I was sincere and must be the genuine article. He said that he had watched, and waited, and realised in the end that I wasn't just 'talking the talk', but was in his opinion also 'walking the walk'. Wow, what a statement to make, I thought, but it's so true. If a person says that he is something then it puts you in the limelight, it's just a matter of time before the truth comes out into the open.

> *'Let your light shine before others, that they may see your good deeds and glorify your Father in heaven.'* Matthew 5:16

He pointed out that I was different from all the other Christians that he'd met inside prison, but he couldn't really figure out what it was until he had personally witnessed what had happened earlier in the kitchen. He told me that he'd started the day in a foul mood. He had sworn that if the opportunity presented itself that he would pulverise the first person that got on his nerves. When he had heard, me singing away in the kitchen he said, 'John, I was wishing it would've been somebody else because I have a lot of respect for you,' but something inside of him had finally snapped and for some reason or other which he couldn't understand he had a sudden urge to seriously hurt me. By this time everybody had stopped working in the kitchen watching and waiting to see what would happen.

You could say that at this stage his reputation was seriously hanging in the balance and he knew that everybody else knew that too. What I heard next was amazing but true because it was also witnessed by many other inmates. He said, 'While I was throwing the beetroots with full force towards your head, it seemed that before they could make contact they miraculously swerved in a different direction either to the left or the right side of you.' While he was sharing this part of the story I remembered a verse in the Bible that I'd previously read and it says, 'He will command his angels concerning you to guard you in all your ways' (Psalm 91:11–12). These verses reminded me also of God's promise that He will protect us from all harm.

He related the rest of his story and said that his frustrations had turned into complete rage. When he had witnessed for himself what was happening, he couldn't help but acknowledge that something spiritual and godly was taking place before his very eyes. Unable to take any more he said that he had walked away and admitted to himself that he was absolutely dumbfounded and confused by all that had happened.

I managed to spend a little time alone with him and I simply explained how much God loved him – even though he had a tough-guy image in prison and a reputation as a fighter – that God knew him through and through. God understood and knew why he was like that and if he allowed God the opportunity to move in his life, then God could help him to change his ways and to become a new person. I was watching his face while we were talking and I noticed that it was getting lighter by the minute and it seemed that all the hardness in his face started to disappear.

Barney had found a new friend that day and, regardless of worrying about what anybody else was thinking about him, he got down on his knees in that small room and gave his heart to Jesus. From that very moment, his life started to change so dramatically that the inmates who'd known him for so long noticed that it was genuine. There were so many changes happening in his life that everybody who knew him realised that a miracle had taken place and they were astounded by this. He became a brilliant witness for Jesus and, over a period of time, he personally brought many other inmates into the faith who also received Jesus into their lives.

*   *   *   *

35

BAPTISED AT LAST!

While I was working in the kitchen I was first introduced to Bill Pilling who oversaw running the kitchen. He was also a Christian and was always smiling and singing Christian songs. I liked him from the moment that I met him and, despite his position as a Principal Officer, we always seemed to get on OK.

One day I was talking with Bill when suddenly he asked whether I'd ever been baptised. I explained that I hadn't and told him what had happened at Wakefield Prison. He didn't say anything else until a few days later when he approached me again, he said that he had been praying about what we had discussed and he felt that God wanted me to make an application through the governor to attend a church outside the prison for the weekend to be baptised.

I laughed at this, and told him that it was very unlikely that this would happen due to my track record and many attempts of trying to escape in the past. He was adamant and said, 'Why don't you just try and see what happens.' I agreed, and he said that he would be praying about it.

The very next day I made the application and soon found myself stood in front of the prison governor. When I walked into his office I was surrounded by prison guards and while he sat there reading through some papers, I was thinking to myself, 'This will never happen.'

After a short while the governor looked at me and made mention about my application and the fact that this was a very unusual request. He made a comment about the length of time that I'd already served and brought home the reality of the time that was still remaining on my sentence. I just started to pray under my breath and asked God to intervene if it was His will that I attend this church to be baptised.

When the governor had finished reading through the application he looked up from his desk and said, 'I can't understand why a Senior Principal Officer would want to take the responsibility of standing surety for you for the day and to take you into his home, but what is even more unusual about this request is that, for some reason that I can't understand, I'm going to allow this application to go through and you will be released into his custody for the day to attend the baptism service.'

I couldn't believe what I was hearing, I knew that this was a direct answer to prayer!

I realised that God had surely intervened on my behalf and for this reason I give Him all the praise and glory.

On the day that I was due to be baptised I cannot explain the way that I was feeling. I'd been waiting for so long to be baptised, that I could never in my wildest dreams imagine it would happen in this way. That morning I was released into Bill's custody and we drove in his car through the countryside until we came to a small town outside Wolverhampton. It was a beautiful day and the sun was shining without a cloud in the sky. We didn't drive straight to the church, but continued through the country lanes until we arrived at this beautiful house. Bill had arranged for me to visit his home and meet his family along with some of his friends before we went to the church.

It was amazing to be in the company of such lovely Christians where everybody was being kind and friendly. At first I found it was quite a strange feeling. I felt that we were worlds apart but, by the grace of God, had been brought together through the faith we shared in Christ Jesus. I tried not to think too much about this at the time and I didn't want it to distract me from thinking of the real reason why I was there: to be baptised and to share a little of my testimony (story) of how I'd become a Christian.

We had a large breakfast at Bill's house and after a short while we all made our way to the church where I was going to be baptised. It was only a small building, seating around 150 people. The meeting started with a time of praise and worship where Christians from all walks of life sang to their hearts' content. It was my first time in a church in the outside world where I was actively taking part in the service. It was so different to the fellowship that I was used to in prison. When the singing had finished I was called onto the platform and was introduced to the congregation by the church pastor who was called Dave; then I received a warm welcome from the whole congregation.

I was a bag of nerves at the beginning, but I started to feel better when I realised that I wouldn't be doing this on my own. There were two other Christians who were also called onto the platform to share their testimony about their faith and the reason why they were getting baptised. The testimonies started. I was last in line and then it came my turn to speak. When I looked into the faces of all those Christians I was feeling even more nervous than ever, when I started to speak I felt that my legs were turning to jelly. I was hoping that nobody would notice my nervousness, but I reminded myself that I'd come this far and I certainly wasn't going to allow my nerves to get the better of me. I spoke for around ten minutes and although I can't remember half of what I spoke about it didn't really matter because I just had an amazing feeling inside that God was looking down and smiling at me.

I was finally baptised in water. I will never forget the experience for as long as I live I did not want this day to end but sadly the service finished. I said my farewells to the church in Wolverhampton and promised that one day I'd return and would speak again. We returned to Bill's home and for the remainder of the day we just laughed and joked around until it was time for me to go back to the prison. Meeting with Bill, his family and all of his friends, I was totally bowled over by the Christian way of life. I said a prayer that day and prayed to God asking that whenever I was released from prison, would it be possible for me to find a church just like that one.

*   *   *   *

36

VISIT FROM AN ANGEL

We arrived back at Featherstone prison at around 8.30pm that day. I needed time alone to think and pray about the day's events. So, I went straight into my cell and closed the door. I got on my knees and I started by praying to God and thanking Him for everything that had been happening in my life. I was feeling so happy inside and I felt that I should share the experience that I'd had with my family. I sat down and started to write a letter to my parents but after a while I realised that I couldn't concentrate on the letter. My mind kept on thinking about the church that I'd attended and while I was trying to write the letter the pages started to become blurred. I guessed I was too tired and decided to finish the letter in the morning.

I thought about reading the Bible for a while instead, but when I picked it up and started to read it I realised after a few minutes that the same thing was happening as had happened with the letter. I couldn't seem to focus on what I was reading because the pages and the writing just seemed to fade into the distance. I didn't realise it at the time but something seemed to be happening around me. There was an air of expectation that was going on inside of me but I didn't know what was going to happen. I felt God's presence in the cell and I can't describe how I was feeling at that time but never in my whole life did

I experience anything like that and feel the way that I did. I decided to turn out the lights and lie on top of my bed for a while to pray and thank God for such a wonderful day.

At around 9.30pm, as I was just lying there with my eyes closed whilst I was praying, I suddenly felt that there was another presence in the room. Everybody was locked into their cells for the night and I hadn't heard the prison guard opening the door. I stopped praying and the moment I opened my eyes I immediately saw an angel standing at the foot of the bed looking directly at me. She was huge in size and the first thing I noticed was that there was a brilliant light coming from all around her. Her face was completely transparent and there was a beautiful and calm glow of light that was coming from her.

I noticed that angel was smiling, and then, suddenly, she began to speak. Except she wasn't actually speaking the words, but singing them. Not only were the words being sung, but they were actually appearing as they came out of the angel's mouth. I couldn't understand what was being sung because I was completely transfixed by what my eyes were seeing. I was looking at the angels' clothes which were glowing in colours of blues and whites that I felt no human eye had ever seen on this earth. I have never seen anything as beautiful as what stood in front of me in that prison cell. She wasn't from this earth and I knew without a doubt that I was in the presence of a heavenly being which we regard as an angel.

I'd not moved an inch and was still lying in the same position when suddenly the words that were flowing from the angel's mouth started to move in my direction. I can't explain it any other way except that I was having a powerful spiritual experience and that for some reason beyond my own understanding I was being visited by an angel of light. The words were in a language that I couldn't understand, but they continued to flow in my direction. Suddenly, an understanding came into my heart and mind and I knew that the words being sung to me were, 'Receive a blessing from your Father.'

I felt myself being lifted off the bed and I noticed that everything around me was disappearing. All the solid, material things in the cell were no longer there and before I realised what was happening I was being lifted through the ceiling of the cell and I found myself looking down at the prison. I could see everything. For a split-second I witnessed a bizarre scene which nobody would believe unless they saw it for themselves. I saw thousands of dark figures, which looked like demons, racing around from cell to cell inside the prison. I could hear weird sounds like cackling and screaming coming from all directions. It was unlike anything that you could think of or imagine – but it was real. I looked on in horror, but then my eyes were turned upwards when I heard a different sound. I could hear singing from above. I felt my body was being lifted higher and I realised that the singing was becoming louder and louder.

I could hear many thousands of voices singing in harmony together and, although I couldn't physically see

181

those that were singing, I knew that I was surrounded by an army of angels. The majestic singing became louder and louder as I was being drawn closer. I soon realised what they were singing and my heart was bursting with excitement and joy because I knew that, for some reason, I was being brought into the very presence of God Himself. Nothing could be compared to what happened next; although it only lasted a moment, I felt that it was for an eternity. I was drawn into this brilliant white light and it became clear that the angels were singing: 'GLORY, GLORY, GLORY TO THE LAMB OF GOD.' I was drawn into this luminous white light and felt as though rivers of living waters were flowing throughout my whole body.

'On the last and greatest day of the festival, Jesus stood and said in a loud voice, "Let anyone who is thirsty come to me and drink. Whoever believes in me, as Scripture has said, rivers of living water will flow from within them."' John 7:37–38

It was as though I was being thoroughly cleansed from all the filthiness of this world. A sudden joy and happiness filled my heart along with a peace and a love which goes beyond all our human understanding. I heard myself singing along with the millions of angels that I was now surrounded by and it was, 'GLORY, GLORY, GLORY TO THE LAMB OF GOD.' I knew that I had been caught up into the heavenly realms and was in the presence of God who is the Creator of everything in the heavens and here on this earth. I wanted to stay there forever but as suddenly as it had started it had finished. Before I realised what was happening I was back in my prison cell and all the material things started to become visible again. I jumped off the bed as though a million volts of electricity had shot through me. I found myself laughing and crying like a little baby. I didn't know what to do next so I just started singing at the top of my voice.

I couldn't help myself at this stage, I felt tears of joy were pouring down my face, my singing went on throughout the night and into the early hours of the morning. That night I didn't sleep for a minute, morning came to quick and I realised that the cell doors were going to be opened at any time. I knew that I couldn't just share this experience that I'd had with just anybody – I'd most probably be committed to an asylum – but I couldn't possibly keep this thing to myself. It's not every day that you see an angel, so I prayed and asked God what I should do next. Then immediately Billy's name came to my mind and I knew that he would understand because he had had a similar experience with God.

At 7.00am the cell doors were opened and like a horse bolting out of the box I shot through them and raced to the other side of the prison. I rushed into Billy's cell; I couldn't contain my excitement. I didn't realise that he was still in bed, but when he looked towards me he had to hide his face under the blankets. I was attempting to explain what had happened, but he pointed out that I didn't have to because it was obvious that I'd spent time in the presence of God because he said that I 'was shining' and the 'Glory of God' was all around me.

After a while we sat down and discussed what had happened. I couldn't really understand why it had happened he explained in simple terms that throughout the Bible in the Old and the New Testament, God had decided to bless some of the people with a visit from Himself or from an angel.

We agreed that it wouldn't be wise to mention this experience to anybody else unless God wanted me to share this with somebody at another time. I found out later from most of the inmates that they had heard my singing throughout the night and normally in a situation like that it would create real difficulties for an inmate who was noisy, especially throughout the whole evening. They explained to me that not one of the inmates would dare to complain because that very night, when they had looked through the bars to find out what the commotion was about, they could see a brilliant white light shining from my prison cell until the early hours of the morning.

*   *   *   *

PART EIGHT

37. THE FIRE SPREADS

The prison Fellowship was growing on a daily basis and there were many men who were giving their lives to Jesus through the testimonies of so many inmates. The governor started to worry about the number of inmates attending the meetings and feared that there may be trouble ahead. He decided to dissolve the meetings and made a rule that only ten men could congregate at any one time on the wings. Usually inmates could cross over from one house to another during association time, but it was announced that we weren't allowed to do that anymore.

The governor didn't realise that by stopping the inmates from meeting together in the evenings it only made matters worse. It was like trying to stamp out a fire with your feet and instead it was spreading it all over the place. The Christians started to get together in their individual houses and within a very short space of time there were prison Christian Fellowship meetings being held in all five of the houses in the prison. Revival was coming to Featherstone at last and there was nothing the governor, the prison guards, or even the prison chaplains could do to put the fire out. Praise the Lord!

God was without a doubt touching many people's lives and there were hundreds of individual prayers being answered on an astronomical level. The fire of God's Holy Spirit spread throughout the prison like a tidal wave. There were no walls thick enough and no prison bars strong enough to stop God from having His way with the prisoners. The Bible says in Luke 4:18 that Jesus came to set the captive free! And countless men were being set free at that time when they called on the name of Jesus. A few weeks later I was called into the office and received the news that I'd be moving shortly to a Category D prison. It was fantastic news and although I was going to miss being a part of what was happening at Featherstone I knew that my time had come to move on and that I was another step closer to finally being released.

*   *   *   *

LEYHILL PRISON

We arrived at the gates of Leyhill and I was shocked to find that there were no walls surrounding the prison. It didn't seem like a prison at all and at first I thought we had taken a wrong turning. But we were in the right place and when we stepped out of the taxi I couldn't help but feel that it was like moving into a residential home in the countryside. It was totally different to Featherstone and all the other prisons that I'd ever been inside. I looked behind me and immediately thought how easy it would be to escape from here. I guess it was just habit that made me think that way because of all the times I'd tried to escape in the past.

I was left at the reception area by myself – which was mind blowing to say the least. I went through the normal prison procedure and was then directed towards a large single-storey building in the grounds. Unescorted I made my way to where I was told to go and came across a small office as I walked through the main doors. It totally blew my mind when I noticed that there was a full-sized snooker table in the larger-than-life recreation room. There was an inmate and a prison officer playing snooker together and laughing like they were best buddies. It was a strange feeling, but I welcomed the peace and tranquillity of what was my new surroundings.

I was greeted by the Principal Officer who said his

name was Jeff who then went on to explain the rules and boundaries of Leyhill. He noticed that I was stood there with total surprise on my face and explained that the rules were different, everybody addressed each other by their first names. It felt as though I was on a holiday camp! When he was finished with the pep talk I was issued with a key for my cell (which was called my 'room') – it nearly bowled me over. It took a while for me to get used to this, the novelty soon wore off and I managed to get the hang of it.

I settled into my new environment and I took full advantage of every opportunity that was available. I started going to the chapel which was separate from the other buildings. It was a great place to spend time away from everybody and to reflect on my life. Also, it was a good opportunity to meet up with the many Christian groups who came to visit the inmates on a regular basis. Life in Leyhill was a lot more relaxed and, even though it was still a prison, I found it was the ideal place for me to prepare myself for the future.

I was introduced to Vic and Sue through the prison fellowship meetings. They were involved with a group of Christians who would regularly visit Leyhill and join in with the praise and worship nights. Once I'd been at Leyhill for eight weeks I was invited to work for them as a gardener over the weekends, which I thoroughly enjoyed.

I also attended their local church which was a real blessing because, apart from my baptism, it was my first proper contact with the church outside the prison.

I received a warm welcome from the whole church and even had the opportunity to share my story with them as I settled into the Christian way of life. I felt totally accepted and loved by these wonderful people, I couldn't wait until I was released from prison so that I could find a church where I belonged. Vic and Sue had two lovely children called Nathan and Emma who accepted me for the person that I was and I didn't feel judged by anybody for what I had done in my past life. I had lots of fun and good memories with this lovely family of Christians who I have remained friends with ever since I've been released from prison.

* * * *

39

BRISTOL HOMELESS

While I was working at doing the gardening on the weekends, I was called into the PO's office and told that there was a possibility that I could work another three days a week in Bristol. I was given a choice of working in a factory or as a volunteer at a Christian drop-in centre. I opted for the latter choice because I felt that I'd rather help people in the community than be stuck in a meaningless job that I wouldn't like doing.

Over the years whilst serving my prison sentence, I completed many courses, all of which could benefit me when I was released, I felt that I was being drawn to work alongside people in the community. I was hopeful that one day I could do something positive with my life and put something back into society rather than take from it. I was introduced to David and Mark who worked together running the centre, and from the moment that I started as a volunteer I knew in my heart that this was where God wanted me to be.

I fitted into the job straight away and I soon found myself helping lots of people from all walks of life. There was such a need amongst the many young adults and older generation that I found it heart breaking to listen to some of their stories. Homelessness and drug addiction was a major problem in that area and sometimes I felt helpless. I continued to build up relationships and friendships with so many that I realised that just listening to their problems and trying to understand them had been a tremendous support to them. I developed a real heart for these people whose lives were so broken that I was challenged in my spirit to pray that God would move in their lives.

My work at the centre started at 9.00am every morning and I would usually be finished by around about 3.00pm. That would leave me about two hours free before the prison bus arrived to take us back to Leyhill. I spent a lot of the time walking around Bristol city centre, and in the underpass, that crossed beneath the motorway I had the opportunity to share my faith about Jesus. This was a place where many prostitutes, drug addicts, and homeless people would congregate. I started to get to know them by name and they would warmly greet me whenever I went to spend time with them. It was an experience that I'll never forget and, as time went by, I realised that this would be the kind of work that I would be involved with when I was finally released from prison.

*　　*　　*　　*

40

THE BLACK AND WHITE CAFE

One day I finished at the centre a couple of hours earlier than usual and I wasn't sure what to do with my spare time. I would normally make my way down to the underpass and spend half an hour there, but it was too early and nobody would've been there at the time. So, I prayed, and I asked God for direction.

It wasn't long before I received an answer and somehow, I felt that God wanted me to walk towards the St Paul's area of Bristol. The previous night I'd watched the news which reported rioting, cars being burnt, police assaults, and stabbings that were going on in the area that night. It certainly was a place of unrest and as I walked through the streets of Bristol I wondered whether I was doing the right thing or not.

I started to feel a little uncomfortable about this, especially when I saw the police riot vans driving around the streets with around a dozen coppers inside; the police helicopter that was constantly flying overhead. I thought to myself that maybe I should call back next week when everything had quietened down, but I felt strongly that I should continue with my journey and see what God wanted me to do.

I started to approach a large bridge. As I got closer I noticed that there were gangs of black and white youths standing around on either side. I had a sports bag that I carried everywhere with me and I thought to myself that I'd better be prepared if there was any trouble ahead. I prayed a quick prayer and asked God to protect me as I continued to walk across the bridge.

Still not knowing the reason why I was there I was soon stopped in my tracks when I was approached by a Rastafarian man who had dreadlocks as long as my arms. He then asked me what I was looking for and said that maybe he could help. I knew the score and what was happening and it was then that I realised that God had brought me all this way just to meet with this young man who stood in front of me. I prayed under my breath and said, 'Well, Lord, I don't know what You want me to say or do, but I'm relying on You to have my back covered if it goes wrong.' I simply turned my attention to the dealer and asked him, 'Well, what have you got?'

He started spitting out a long list of stuff that he had to sell which almost sounded poetical. It reminded me of being in Moss Side in Manchester when I was younger. He said, 'Well, man, I've got da weed, I've got da speed, I've got da smack, and I've got da crack,' and it was while he was saying all this that God spoke to me and said, 'I want you to tell him that I understand what he's going through and for him not to worry because God still loves him.' It was one of those moments when I thought to myself, 'Well, Lord, if that's You speaking then no harm will come to me. And if it isn't from You, God, then I could be thrown over the bridge and end my days here on this earth right now.'

He had finished rapping and he seemed quite pleased with himself that he'd completed his spiel without a break. I thought, 'Well, Lord, here goes,' and I looked him squarely in the eyes and said, 'Look, bro', it sounds great but I have something inside my bag here which is about a million times as powerful as what you've got to sell.' I hesitated for a moment because at this stage he was looking all around him suspiciously. A couple of his mates had overheard what I was saying and were making their way towards us. I continued, and said, 'Not only is it better than all the stuff that you've got combined, but let me tell you something: it's absolutely FREE!'

I was surrounded by this time and everybody was staring intently at my sports bag which I had started to pull from my shoulder. I opened it up and retrieved my King James Version of the Bible from inside. The minute they noticed that it wasn't drugs they soon lost interest and went back to their positions on the bridge. I looked at the Rastafarian who was stood there with his mouth wide open. For a minute, I thought that I was going to be killed. So, I quickly said, 'Listen, I'm here because God has specifically brought me to this place to pass on a message to you directly from Him.' I told him what God had told me to say and while I was speaking I noticed there were tears flowing from his eyes. It was obvious that this was a godly thing that was happening because when I said that God still loved him, he completely broke down and started to cry.

I wasn't watching his friends who were looking over, but I knelt beside him and started to pray quietly.

A couple of minutes passed before he could speak and when he did I was really touched by what he said. He finally stood up and took both my hands in his and said, 'My mother is a born-again Christian and she has been praying for me for years. When I woke up this morning, the last thing she said to me was that she will be praying that I'll meet up with a man of God on the street today who will speak God's word directly into my heart.' He said that at this point he had just walked out of the house, and had even laughed at her with his friends, something he had done many times in the past.

I managed to pray with this young man that day on the bridge who promised that he would attend church that week with his mother. I'd never been to St Paul's before and I didn't know anybody in that area. But, I do know that God was right there beside me, and when I passed on the message it built a new bridge of friendship between two complete strangers who had never met before. My new friend introduced himself as Jeff and said that he wanted to introduce me to some friends of his. I followed him. While we were talking, together there were lots of passing cars screeching around the streets causing havoc with the police. I noticed that there were gangs of youths hanging around, wearing scarves and hoodies; they were stood around on almost every street corner with bricks and loaded bottles of petrol in their hands.

Amazingly, I had no sense of danger towards myself and trusted that God was protecting me through thick and thin. We finally arrived at a café in St Paul's which was called the Black and White Café. I thought we were going inside for a coffee but when we entered the premises I think a cup of coffee was the last thing on my mind. I was the only white man in there; it appeared that we had walked into the headquarters of a warzone. The café was packed out. Everybody stopped talking and looked in my direction but when they noticed that I was with Jeff the atmosphere relaxed a little.

He disappeared for a while and when he returned he announced to everybody that I was his friend and that I was an evangelist who had a story to tell. For the next half, an hour I was able to share my testimony with around about thirty men who listened intently. After sharing my story, I spoke about Jesus. It was through meeting with Jeff on that bridge earlier that I was now accepted and given free rein to walk around St Paul's without any harm coming to me. I was also introduced to some of the biggest gangsters and drug dealers in Bristol who, over the next few weeks while I became familiar with the surroundings, would stop and talk for a while whenever I was in the area.

One day I met with a black guy who was walking down the street with his eleven-year-old son. He was obviously struggling to walk straight. I learnt that he'd had a serious car accident previously which had rendered him almost crippled in his legs, lower back and shoulders. I witnessed to him about the healing power of Jesus, and asked whether it would be all right to pray for him. He didn't see a problem and welcomed the idea. I knelt in the street and laid hands on his legs, which were in most pain, and I prayed that God would heal his body from the feet upwards. I didn't think any more of it and went about my business that day, stopping and talking with people about Jesus.

About a month later, when I was walking down the same street, I heard somebody shouting my name. When I turned around I saw that this man was running towards me. I thought that I recognised him vaguely but I couldn't figure out exactly who it was until he threw his arms around me in front of everybody. It was Noel who I 'd prayed for recently and I realised that there was something different about him. He told me that when he went home on the day that I prayed for him, he started to feel a tingling sensation all over his body and it had lasted all throughout the night.

When he woke up the next day he said that he didn't feel any pain in his body whatsoever, and when he realised what was happening he had thrown himself on the floor and had given thanks to God for healing his body. It was a fantastic day and when he went on his way word soon spread around that the evangelist who prayed for him was to be respected as a true man of God.

I wasn't used to being popular anywhere but every time I walked around the St Paul's area of Bristol I always felt as safe as houses. I found myself being stopped in the street by people I didn't even know who just wanted to say hello, or ask for prayers.

*   *   *   *

41

THE FORBIDDEN FRUIT

While I was working at the Christian drop in centre I met a beautiful girl called Eve. She was an ex-model and had come down from London to live near her family in Bristol. We seemed to click straight away and it wasn't long before she started to visit me at Leyhill. We wrote to each other every day for several months and she would visit me as often as she could. We fell in love with each other and we talked about getting married when I was released from prison. It was a fantastic feeling that we had for each other, which I believe neither of us wanted to go away. But there was one little problem: she wasn't a Christian.

We discussed this together and she said that she wasn't really interested in Christianity, but was willing to get married anyway. In the Bible, it says that we must not be 'unequally yoked' together because a relationship between a Christian and a non-Christian usually didn't work out, but I was willing to overlook this because my feelings for her were so strong. I felt that she was a true blessing from God and it didn't matter to me that she wasn't a Christian because I felt that eventually we could work something out about this. My Christian friends tried to warn me about the possibility of being in a wrong relationship, but I just wouldn't listen. As far as I was concerned we were going to get married and that was it.

I never believed in prison romances from the start. I'd met hundreds of inmates over the years who had got themselves involved in a relationship while they were inside prison and 99.9 per cent of the time the relationship ended up not working out. It was because I was a Christian that I knew that God had plans for my life but now that I found myself in that same situation it seemed that God's plans were being put on the back burner for a while. I had big hopes, dreams, and ambitions for the future, but it didn't cross my mind that by getting involved with Eve it could prevent me from fulfilling the calling that God had on my life. I really struggled with this and I prayed hard that God would bless us together. His answer was not what I expected. And, it came sooner rather than later.

There was an evening Christian meeting held at the chapel in Leyhill. I had heard that there was a group of Christians that had travelled all the way from Africa to share an amazing story of adventure, danger and death in the villages and townships where they lived and worked. It sounded quite interesting so I decided that I would attend the meeting later when I had finished writing letters to my family and friends.

When I went to the chapel in the evening I noticed that there were around thirty inmates already sitting around and waiting for the speakers to arrive. I thought to myself that this was going to be an interesting evening. What I hadn't realised was that God had brought this small group of people all the way from Africa to pass on a direct message to me about my relationship with Eve.

The small group had arrived and after they were formerly introduced the meeting got underway. The speaker wasted no time, before he started he said that he believed that God had wanted him to share something with a particular person in the meeting before he shared his story.

He said that he didn't understand why but God had wanted him to speak firstly about how they usually caught orang-utans in their part of Africa. He explained that they were classed as one of the most stubborn animals on earth and, in order to catch them, they would find a place where they would dig a hole in the ground. When the hole was deep enough they would place a large jar into the earth with a narrow neck sticking out at the top. They would then cover around the edges with soil, drop a sweet delicacy into the jar, then hide and wait.

After a while the unsuspecting animal would detect the aroma of the delicacy and would be drawn in the direction of the smell. It would then attempt to put its hand into the top of the jar. Eventually it would realise that its hand was far too big to reach inside. Then it would use another tactic: by squeezing its hand together it would practically force it into the jar. Once this had happened, the orang-utan would then reach down to the bottom and grab the delicacy. It would automatically clench its fist around the sweet and would not release its grip. Try as it might, it wouldn't be possible to free itself from the jar unless it let go of the prize that it had such a firm grip on. It was a cunning technique that was generally used and worked in capturing this animal in the wild, it was because the orang-utans were such stubborn animals that their reluctance to release the sweet would result in there finally being captured.

As the speaker was sharing this part of the story I was starting to feel a little uncomfortable because I had a sinking feeling that it was speaking directly into my situation. I started fidgeting in the meeting and really wanted to leave, but I stayed to hear this man out.

He finished the story by telling how they would sneak up from behind this large animal and would bop it over the head with a weapon, immobilising the orang-utan and rendering it unconscious. It had lost its freedom through pure ignorance and stubbornness. At this point I started to realise that God was definitely speaking directly to me about my relationship with Eve. I tried to shrug the feeling off and left the meeting without saying anything to anybody. When I arrived back on the wing and closed the door of my cell I had that sinking feeling that God wasn't going to let this one pass by and, as much as I wanted Him to forget about it, I knew that He wouldn't.

I knew by now that God was warning me that I was in a relationship that wasn't part of His plan for my life. But I was being even more stubborn and even tried to argue with Him about it. I didn't want to end things with Eve and pleaded with God to bless the relationship. But it never happened. I didn't sleep much that night because I couldn't get it out of my mind. I knew that I had to finish the relationship but I guess I was being as stubborn as that old orang-utan.

When I woke up the next day I got ready to go into Bristol and was looking forward to meeting up with Eve.

We had spoken the night before and had arranged to meet together in Bristol where the prison bus stopped off in the city centre. It was a frosty morning and while I was waiting for the bus to arrive I looked out of the window and saw a cobweb that was positioned in the top right-hand corner. I watched it for a while and noticed that a daddy-longlegs had got caught up in the web and was struggling to break itself free. I also noticed that not far away, tucked away in the corner, there was a big black spider who seemed to be waiting for the daddy-longlegs to run out of strength before he dashed forward and spun a web around it, rendering it completely helpless. I had a thought and said to myself, 'If I wanted, I could reach out of the window and set that daddy-longlegs free.' That's when I heard God's voice very clearly and distinctly when He said, 'That's just what I can do for you too!'

I waited for more, but not another word was spoken. I knew from that moment what I had to do and, strangely enough, even though I felt sad inside, I also felt a tremendous peace about it all. I prayed and asked God whether it would be possible for Him to speak with Eve before I met with her that morning. I had a feeling that she would be really upset but I knew that I was making the right decision. The prison bus arrived and, all the way on the journey to the city centre, I sat at the back praying. When we arrived, I saw her car which was parked along the roadside. Ten minutes later we found ourselves walking along the harbour. I was dreading what to say to her and I lifted a final prayer before I found the courage and said, 'I have something to tell you . . .' But before I could continue she stopped me in my tracks and said, 'Before you speak, I've got something to tell you too.'

She told me about something that had happened with her the night before. She said that when she went to sleep that night she had a dream, and in that dream God had appeared to her and told her that we mustn't get married because He had plans for my life. I looked at her with astonishment in my eyes because I realised that at the exact time that she had the dream I was praying for her in my cell. I told her my side of the story too and amazingly she took it quite well. We both seemed to have a deep understanding about this and for the rest of the day we talked and laughed together like two little kids. Eventually we had to leave each other, but we hugged and parted as best friends.

You may be asking yourself why I've mentioned this in my book. Well, I think it's important and I just want you to know that God can speak to you in many ways. That when he does He can use all means that are necessary for you to get the message. In my case God spoke in three distinct ways concerning my relationship with Eve: one was through the Christians who travelled all the way from Africa to pass on a word from God; another was hearing God's voice very distinctly as I watched the spider and its prey while I stood in my cell waiting for the prison bus; finally, when He even appeared to a non-Christian in a dream and gave her a specific word for a specific reason.

I've realised from that experience that when God is trying to get your attention, it's really important that when we hear His voice we should be obedient to what He's saying. Not long after we separated Eve made a decision in her own heart and accepted Jesus into her life, although we never rekindled our relationship, we are still to this day the best of friends. If I had continued to pursue a life with Eve I strongly believe that I would never have been able to fulfil the calling on my life. I thank God that He decided to intervene on my behalf at that time because it wouldn't be possible for me to share in my next book about the exciting new life that I've lived since being released from prison.

*   *   *   *

PART NINE

42. RELEASED FROM PRISON

I was finally released from prison on the 17th of December 1992. I'd served six years and two months of my ten-year sentence. It was a great feeling to walk outside those prison gates after spending so much time inside. I had experienced this feeling previously on other sentences but this time I knew that things weren't going to be the same. I didn't know what the future held but I knew in my heart that things were definitely going to be different because now I had God in my life.

I returned to Manchester to live at my parents' home with the hope that I could find work and somewhere to live for myself and son Jason, who had been waiting all those years for his dad to come and collect him. It was an exciting day and when the train arrived at Manchester Piccadilly station my parents were waiting to meet me on the platform along with my eight-year-old son. It was something that I had been dreaming of for a very long time and now it had become a reality.

When I arrived at my parents' home all my family members were there waiting. They had stood by me throughout my prison sentence and at long last they were relieved that this ordeal had come to an end. I didn't realise then, but later I would find out that a different kind of ordeal was about to begin in my life.

We partied through the night and the following few weeks seemed like one big party. I visited family members during that time and each one was just as excited that I was finally home. They also arranged a welcome home party at their houses. So, for a period of time it seemed all that was happening in my life was that I was out drinking and partying all the time.

None of my family were Christians and even though they could see that I had changed significantly they just couldn't understand what I was going through. I desperately wanted my brothers and sisters and especially my mum and dad to come to know Jesus in the same way that I did. But all my efforts and attempts to see this happen just fell on deaf ears. It seemed that they were too set in their ways. Even though they were glad that I had become a Christian, they weren't really interested in hearing about God or the Church. They were too busy living out their own lives and were quite happy to continue living it without bringing God into the equation.

I was feeling quite despondent about this but I was determined not to let it affect my faith in God. With the partying lifestyle over I started attending a church in the local area. It was a very lively church and I was made to feel really welcome but something at the back of my mind kept niggling at me. Even though I was having fellowship with other Christians, something kept saying to me that I didn't belong there. I was constantly reading my Bible and praying to God and asking Him for direction.

At the same time, I was having difficulties at home with my son Jason. When I first went into prison he was just starting to walk, and when I was finally released he was nearly eight years of age. I'd never imagined how difficult it would be to raise a child on your own. For years, I imagined myself treating my son as my best friend where we would never fall out or argue about the silly things in this life. But I was in for a rude awakening because I never imagined how difficult things would be when I was finally confronted with that responsibility.

Even though I had my family around me at the time to help and give their support, I knew that every decision that I had to make was solely my responsibility. It was a shock to the system because this was something that I wasn't used to at all. All the responsibility and decisions had been made for me during the time that I was in prison. I didn't have to worry about anything until I was released into the outside world. Suddenly I was faced with the responsibility of not only being a single parent but also of taking on the full responsibility of being a father and provider to an eight-year-old boy whom I didn't really know.

Jason had great expectations from me when I was released from prison, I didn't realise that he had plans of his own which I wasn't aware of at the time. He wanted to spend every waking moment with his dad – which was understandable under the circumstances. He loved the attention he was receiving from everybody and we had some great times together, but I was desperate to find employment and I just couldn't be there for him like he was expecting. I tried to sit down and have a serious conversation with my son but he was only a child and no matter how hard I tried to explain the situation to him, he just didn't seem to understand. I even treated him like a little adult this was a big mistake on my part because what I should've realised was that Jason was just a small boy who couldn't possibly understand or appreciate the things that happen in the adult world.

He started to misbehave when he thought he wasn't getting his own way, and this made things difficult with my parents. I was looking for work one day when I received a call to come home as soon as possible. When I arrived both my parents were sitting in the living room with desperate expressions on their faces. I found out that while Jason was upstairs he had been playing around with a cigarette lighter and had set a duvet cover alight in the bedroom. I was really shocked at this and ran upstairs to deal with the matter. I remember I was shouting very loudly at my son who was terrified to see his dad behaving this way. I could hardly control myself from hitting him.

It was a real nightmare and I thought to myself that I'd most probably made a mistake in bringing him home to live with us. I felt really guilty about raising my voice but I was horrified to think that he could've burnt my parents' home down, killing himself and everybody inside. I'd only been out of prison for a few weeks and it seemed as though my life was falling in all around me. The responsibility of being a lone parent who couldn't find work due to my criminal record was starting to take its toll, I started to feel the pressure. I could feel the temptation of my past life burning at my heels; I knew I only had to make a phone call and I'd have a different kind of work. I was adamant that I wasn't going to go down that road ever again. I couldn't forget what God had done for me while I was inside prison and I strongly believed that God was right there beside me even though things were looking difficult at the time.

It was a real test of my faith and there were times when I felt that I was being stretched beyond the limits, but I remembered what it said in the Bible about how God wouldn't let you be tested beyond what you could endure (1 Corinthians 10:13). I held on to that promise and prayed for God to help. I knew that whatever happened I had to put my trust in God with every decision. I made myself, a promise that from thereon it would be God who would have to help me to make the right decisions. I prayed about my future and although God had promised me a whole new way of life I realised that I had to play my part in making it work. I had to make the right decisions not just for myself, but for my son also because I knew that whatever I decided to do from that moment would affect his life too. I remembered all those Scriptures that I'd read in the Bible and started to speak them into my life.

Although my family were being very supportive in lots of ways they had their own lives to live too, and their own families to support without having to worry about my problems. I didn't know how to handle this situation so in desperation I turned to God once again and prayed for Him to help me find work. It was a week later that I finally found employment working in an

Italian restaurant called Da Vinci's in Manchester city centre. I was working shift work as a kitchen porter, which didn't pay too well, but it was a start, and it did help at home with the finances. I worked there for two months, during which time I continued going to the Christian Centre which was just around the corner from my parents' house.

I was sat at home one day talking with my parents about God. I was trying to explain the difference between the kind of faith that they had in God and the kind of faith that I had, but it was like flogging a dead horse. Both my parents were strong-believing Catholics but apart from attending the occasional wedding or funeral they never really took their faith seriously enough to go to church or read the Bible. I tried to point out that the pictures of Pope John Paul or the crucifix on the wall weren't enough to get them into heaven and that even though they professed to believe in God it wasn't enough. I explained that the difference between the God that they believed in and the God that I believe in was that their God was plastered all around the walls and the God that I believe in is living inside my heart.

I continued attending the Christian Centre, but I couldn't shake off the feeling that I wasn't meant to be in that place and was praying for God to show what His will was for my life. I knew that while I was in prison God had said that He wanted me to go down to the south of England. I wasn't exactly sure where in the South that He wanted me move to, but I just knew in my heart that that's where He wanted me to be. I started to feel depressed about my failure to make things work and as a result I started to turn to drink. I was desperately trying to distance myself from my old way of life but I felt as though I was being drawn back in time and that I'd already failed miserably. I knew that God had done a miracle in my life, but I also knew that if I was to live this new life that He promised then this would need 100% commitment from me to make it work. I asked myself, where should I start?

*   *   *   *

43

BREAKTHROUGH!

My breakthrough came when, one day, my dad sat me down and expressed his concern about my drinking and behaviour. I'd been drinking heavily and was constantly feeling depressed about my situation. I felt trapped inside and feared that I'd missed out on the opportunity to start a new life. I couldn't see a way out of my situation, that morning dad gave me the golden opportunity. He reminded me of my desire to move down south and offered to pay my coach fare that same day. I knew that he was right in what he was saying and I broke down and cried out in desperation. I ran upstairs and started to pray to God. I prayed like I'd never prayed before and asked God to give me direction. I had dreamt of this day, but I didn't want to make the mistake of taking my son away from school to a place I knew nothing about.

When I prayed, I asked God to provide me with a job and a decent school for my son Jason to attend. I also prayed for God to provide us with somewhere to live when we moved down south. It was a big decision, but I had to do something about my situation. If I stayed in Manchester I knew that I was going to sink back into my old ways. I discussed this with my parents and it was decided that I would leave Jason with them and travel on the coach that same day. I took my dad up on his offer and by mid-afternoon I was sat on a coach travelling to Torquay in the south of England.

When I arrived in Torquay I felt as though a weight had been lifted from my shoulders. I prayed and asked God to show me the way and, although I didn't know a soul in this part of the world, I just knew things weren't ever going to be the same.

Before I set off from Manchester I'd been given the phone number of a Christian called David who helped ex-offenders when they were released from prison. I rang the number as soon as I arrived at the coach station but there was no answer. I didn't know what to do next so I just sat in a café and drank coffee for a while.

I waited, and waited, and rang the number again, but there was still no answer. I started to panic because I didn't have an address and I didn't know where this man lived. I felt like a complete stranger in a new town but then I remembered God's promise in His word that He would never leave me and that if I were to ask anything in His name then He would give it to me (John 14:13–14). I prayed in that little café and asked the Holy Spirit (God!) to show me what to do next. I felt a real peace come over me and, before I realised it, I was walking away from the bus station towards the nearest housing estate. I didn't know where I was going but I felt that God was leading me in the right direction. About half an hour later I found myself standing in front of a house in Wrights Lane. I wasn't sure what to do next. Even though I felt a little foolish I eventually plucked up the courage and knocked on the front door . . . and waited.

A man wearing overalls answered the door, looking as though he'd just come home from work. He looked at me for a moment and then asked, 'Can I help you?' I know it sounds crazy but I said the first thing that came to mind and replied, 'God has sent me.' There was silence for a moment but then he laughed and said, 'Well, you'd better come in!' It just happened that the very person I was trying to phone earlier at the bus station was the very same man who was standing in front of me. It was an amazing coincidence, but it's true. I stayed at Dave's house for a week and while I was there he showed me where the local job centre and housing association was located. Also, I was introduced to the headmaster of a primary school in Barton for my son Jason. So, within that short period of time while I stayed at his house, it seemed that all my prayers had been answered. I found a job, somewhere to live, and a fantastic school for my son.

It was the beginning of an exciting new journey in my life. I returned to Manchester and shared the good news with my family, who were delighted. It was the break that we were all waiting for, I wasn't going to miss out on this opportunity. A week later I was on a train to Torquay with my son Jason and we were ready to start our new life down south. It was a scorching hot summer's day and I remember while we were travelling on the train that we both had smiles on our faces that were so wide we looked like a couple of Cheshire cats. I didn't care, and although I was unsure about what the future held I just knew in my heart that everything was going to be all right.

I've now lived in Torbay for twenty years and my life has been a real rollercoaster of a ride – but that is something I will share with you when I write my second book, which is called' Staying Out'.

*   *   *   *

PART 10

44. IN CLOSING

It is possible for you to be completely set free from your past life and it's never too late to change no matter who you are or what you've done. There is light at the end of the tunnel for everybody and I just want you to know that, regardless of where you are right now and despite what you've done in the past, 'JESUS LOVES YOU' and 'HAS FORGIVEN YOU!' He has a whole new way of life waiting for you outside when you are released from prison. I know from personal experience that God will never let you down and, to you, my friends, that's the message that I want to leave with you. Please give God that opportunity to show His love for you and invite Jesus into your hearts. I guarantee that you will never regret making that decision.

In reading my story you may be asking yourself the question, 'Is it true?' And, 'If God is real, then what about me?' That's the question I think we should all be asking ourselves when we are faced with the truth for the first time. It is undoubtedly true that God truly does love you and is waiting for you to give Him the opportunity to prove this to you. I believe it's vitally important that you come to the place where a decision has to be made in your lives. If you are completely honest with yourself and accept that your situation is without hope, it will make things much easier and will help you to make the right decision which will move you in the right direction.

I have never met an inmate who wanted to be in prison but if you're one of those inmates who have become institutionalised throughout your life and depend on the prison system to be the source of your security, I just want you to know that there is another way and that is through Jesus. I'd heard about God's unfailing love by reading somebody else's story; that His love was demonstrated through His Son Jesus when He died on the cross for our sins. I desperately needed to know whether it was true or not, which took me on my journey. The Bible says that if anybody should seek after the truth then they will find it, and when you find it 'THE TRUTH WILL SET YOU FREE!'

*   *   *   *

Without a doubt, there is much more to life than this and if you want to find out more than I would encourage you to step into the loving arms of Jesus. Stop for a minute and think about where you are right now and ask yourself the question: Is there any likelihood that your life is going to change without divine intervention?

I was totally honest with myself, and I knew in my heart that even though I knew that I could maybe change a few small things in my life, I could never change myself enough to break away from the lifestyle that I was living. I needed a miracle and that's exactly what happened. The same could be said for you, my friend. You need a miracle in your life, too, and only with God's help can this happen.

God understands exactly what you're going through right at this moment and no matter who you are, or where you've been, He knows everything about you because He is the Creator and we are part of His creation. The Bible says that He knew you before you were born. It's incredible to think about this, but it's so true. God knows every hair that's on your head and I think if God can pay so much attention to such a minute detail then He's worth listening to. Don't let this opportunity pass you by and, whatever you do, please don't try and be the tough guy (or girl) by saying that you don't need God. I believe that everybody has a heart and when God breaks through the stones which are built around it, it never ceases to amaze Him when He finds that precious stone within.

I know what you're going through because I've been where you are. I messed up like you, and I made many mistakes in life with disastrous consequences. I've been to the end of the line and can honestly say that without God's help I would still be living without hope or any real purpose for living. I've been completely delivered and set free from my addiction to drugs, and since I've been released from prison my whole life has been completely transformed and turned around. I'm excited for you as you read this book because I know that if you've been challenged by what you've read, then you're about to make that most important decision and discovery for yourself. You are going to make that decision to allow God to change your life for the better.

God knows everything about you, and He has heard everything that you have ever said in this life. Most importantly, He's seen everything that you've done. Nobody's perfect, my friend, and God knows that too. When we eventually die, and leave this earth we will be brought before God and will be judged on that great day of judgement when He will judge the whole world. We all deserve to be punished because we are full of sin, but the punishment can be avoided for those who acknowledge God and receive forgiveness through His son Jesus. You might be asking, 'But what must I do to make things right?' and I'll say to you that with this attitude in mind 'YOU'RE CLOSER TO YOUR MIRACLE THAN YOU THINK!'

The worst thing that you can do right now is to hear about the truth and to do absolutely nothing with it. Millions of people are searching for something in this life and there are millions of people who are discovering the amazing truth of God's word around the world and they are being set free. Without a doubt, for you to become a Christian it means that you have decided to follow Jesus and to live a new life that He's promised to those who believe. It says in the Bible that God's ways are different to ours and that by choosing God's way I want you to know that you're on a winner.

I'm sure that if there was another way, millions of people would have found it by now. The Bible specifically states that there is no other way to the Father (God) except through the Son (Jesus). You can experience God for yourself and find out this amazing truth by simply asking Jesus to reveal himself to you and for you to take that first step of faith by inviting Him to come and live in your heart. It's as easy as ABC. You might be saying to yourself, 'But I hate religion,' and I'll agree with you because I feel the same way. Personally, I think that everybody hates religion in some form or another because of all the problems that it's caused all around the world. Amazingly enough, God feels the same way too, but Christianity is NOT about religion. It's about being in a relationship with God through the power of His Holy Spirit. Jesus has made it possible for us to know the Father who created you and the whole world.

I didn't become a Christian by going to a church building once or twice a week. I became a Christian because I'd heard about the truth and I genuinely wanted to know whether it was real or not. The Bible says that if you seek after the truth, you will find it. And that's just what I did, my friend, and it's something that I'm hoping and praying that you will do too. I was on a mission and I didn't care about what other people felt or thought about me when I was reading the Bible in prison. I had more important things to think about – what was going to happen with the rest of my life and what did the future hold for somebody like me. I made the decision to turn away from my old life and decided to follow Jesus.

What's even more amazing is what it says in the Bible about what happens when you find the truth. It clearly states in John 8:32 that 'You will know the truth, and the truth will set you free'! There's nothing on this earth that can be compared to what God has in store for you. There's no amount of booze, drugs, or money that can compensate for the life that you're missing out on. It's about time you started getting real with yourself and admit the truth about yourself: that you are simply lost without Him. I believe that you've read this book for a reason and that you've continued reading it because you are hungry for the truth. The Bible says that if you seek after the truth you will find it, and when you do THE TRUTH WILL SET YOU FREE!

My friend, please don't keep looking for excuses; you've already missed out on so much that God has got to give you. It's not too late for you! and I know that there's no sin in your life that God can't forgive you for. I've told my story to hundreds of people over the years since becoming a Christian and have helped many people to make a simple decision in their lives to accept Jesus into their hearts. It says in the Bible, in Revelation 3:20, that Jesus is standing knocking at the door of your heart, and saying, 'Let me in.' He won't force Himself to come into your heart because that will make Him like a thief. There is only one way to do this and that is that you must acknowledge Him and admit that you're a sinner. Your sin separates you from having that relationship with God and the only way that you can break the atmosphere is when you simply turn to God and ask for His forgiveness!

I understand that life can sometimes seem harsh and that you may be feeling that you've drawn the short straw, but everything could change for you. I've been where you are right now and maybe further than you can imagine. I want you to know that whatever you're going through at this time, and no matter how you feel about your situation, God is bigger than your circumstances and He is the solution to your problems. If you are continually looking for excuses, then you're not being honest with yourself. I am speaking to you with all sincerity and honesty, and would encourage you with all my heart to at least give it a try. WHAT HAVE YOU GOT TO LOSE? Let me tell you that you've got nothing to lose . . . but everything to gain.

Firstly, you must ask Jesus to come and live in your heart. The Bible says that you've just got to say 'sorry' to God – it's as easy as that! – and He will forgive you for everything that you've done. You don't have to say ten 'Hail Mary's and all that stuff. Simply turn to God wherever you are right now and admit that you've done wrong and He will not only forgive you for your sins but He will also give you a clean slate. He will give you a NEW LIFE with a NEW HOPE and a NEW FUTURE. He will introduce you to His friends and His family within the church and around the world. You will no longer be reliant and dependent on mind-bending drugs, and you will experience a whole new way of life when HE SETS YOU FREE!

If you are serious and want to know Jesus as your Lord and Saviour, all I ask from you is that you repeat this prayer out loud and, after doing that, please link up with other Christians, wherever you are, and share what you've just done. It's a simple prayer, but at the same time it's a life-changing prayer for you. I believe with all my heart that God is waiting for you to say this prayer and is ready to move heaven and earth to meet with you where you are. But, it must be a genuine and sincere prayer that comes from your heart. I can promise you that you will never regret making that decision and can guarantee that your life will change around for the better and will never be the same again.

Dear Lord Jesus,

Thank you for dying on the cross in my place. You gave yourself up and took the punishment that I deserve, because of your sacrifice, I believe it has wiped away ALL of my sins. I know I've lived my life without You right up until now, but I want to change that, and I decide to follow You, Lord. I acknowledge You are the Son of God, and that without You, I will be going to a worse place, called Hell.

Please, take a hold of my life from this very moment, and make me into a better person. I need to change, but I know deep down inside that I can't do this all by myself. So, I'm taking my first real step of faith and I'm relying on you to make it work. I invite you Holy Spirit to come and live inside of me, and for You, Lord Jesus, to take Your rightful place in my heart and to be the Lord of my life.

I'm trusting you right now, and will take you up on your promise that You will never leave me, nor forsake me, and I believe You will lead me into a better life than where I'm at.

I desperately need You right now, so please, dear God, help me as I call out to You! I've heard that You baptise people with your Holy Spirit, and as I am now Your child and I belong to you, please help me to receive the baptism of Your Holy Spirit!

Thank You, Lord Jesus, for loving me!

If you have made this decision and you think that it would help if you had somebody to write to you, I am willing to arrange for other Christians to contact you. If you want to write and share your story after reading this book I promise you that I will read all your letters and will pray for you if you're still in prison. I look forward to hearing from you and pray that God will bless you as you start on this exciting new journey in your life.

*   *   *   *

END NOTE FROM THE AUTHOR

My hope is that this book find itself being read by many hundreds if not thousands of male and female inmates and their families around the country and the world.

It doesn't matter, who you are, where you come from or where you've been in life – I just want you to know that Jesus Christ loves you and He died for you so that you may be free.

If you've read this book and been encouraged by the testimony that you've heard and would like support the book with financial blessing, I can be contacted by email:

insideout@rivieracc.org.uk

Or you can send letters to:
Riviera Christian Centre,
Hodson Close,
Paignton,
Devon,
TQ3 3NU